The Un-Bunny Book

The Un-Bunny Book

Kathy Widenhouse

These pages may be copied.

Permission is granted to the buyer of this book to
photocopy student materials for use
with children in Bible teaching.

LEGACY PRESS®

To Donna McNally and the volunteers at Smithville United Methodist
Church in Dunkirk, Maryland, who made our Easter Fun Day a reality.

THE UN-BUNNY BOOK
Copyright ©2003 by Legacy Press
ISBN 1-58411-028-7
Legacy reorder# LP48031
church and ministry/ministry resources/children's ministry

Legacy Press
P.O. Box 261129
San Diego, CA 92196

Illustrator: Chuck Galey
Cover Illustrator: Court Patton

Printed in the United States of America

Contents

What is The Un-Bunny Book?

For Christians, Easter is the most important holiday of the year. It is a time of great joy as we come together to celebrate Jesus' resurrection and our new life in Him. Yet in our communities, there are relatively few children's events at Easter time, especially compared to Christmas. In particular, there is an absence of family activities that point to the true meaning of Easter.

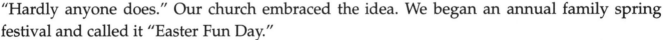

During the spring my daughter turned 3, I looked for activities to help her learn about Easter. Within the 20-mile radius of my home, I found only two: she could meet the Easter Bunny at a local appliance store one Saturday afternoon, or she could hunt for eggs with 100 other frenzied kids at a county park on Easter Monday. The frustration of that experience became the inspiration for *The Un-Bunny Book.*

"We should host a special program for children at Easter," I told my church board shortly thereafter. "Hardly anyone does." Our church embraced the idea. We began an annual family spring festival and called it "Easter Fun Day."

Our Easter Fun Day shows kids and parents that Jesus' resurrection is something to celebrate. During a two-hour time frame, youngsters ages 3 through 12 make crafts, play games, hunt for eggs, and most importantly, hear and learn the Easter story.

The event will create a tremendous opportunity for your church to reach into the community for Jesus. Christians who attend find that it revitalizes their faith and readies them for Holy Week. Unchurched visitors see the Gospel in action. And children of all ages learn that Easter is about more than chicks and chocolate – it is really about a miraculous, empty tomb. In fact, the program embodies the command in Psalm 9:11: "Sing praises to the Lord…proclaim among the nations what He has done."

Ways to Use this Book

An event at your church. Whether you are a first-time volunteer or a seasoned Christian education professional, this book can help you organize a Bible-based Easter event for families. It will take you step-by-step through what you need to do to get started, plan, set up and follow-up a successful celebration for children in your community. There are detailed instructions for each activity, and reproducible patterns and checklists to make your job easier.

continued on next page

 **Children's ministries.** All games, crafts and snacks in this book are based on Scripture. Use them to underscore a Sunday school lesson during Lent or to organize an evening of fun for your Bible club.

The *Scripture Reference Index* on page 167 shows where to turn for a hands-on activity that emphasizes a specific Bible verse or portion of the Easter story.

Party and Lesson Themes on pages 20-22 sort the book's activities according to events and topics related to Easter. This chart can help you create a Sunday school lesson or personalize your existing curriculum.

 **Children's sermons.** Pastors and children's workers can turn to ready-made *Lessons for Children's Church* starting on page 104 as they prepare to communicate the Easter message to youngsters. Other activities in this book can be adapted into object lessons, too.

 At home. Many families have long-standing Christmas traditions but have few for Easter. This book can help you develop activities that bring special meaning to you and your children each spring. Learn how to plan an Easter party for the kids in your neighborhood. Use the patterns and ideas to decorate your home in anticipation of the Resurrection. Make special refreshments from the Snacks section during Lent. Set aside a Saturday afternoon to play the Easter games with your children. Re-enact the Easter story!

"He is not here; He has risen." (Matthew 28:6). Turn the page to learn how to start communicating that wonderful truth to children and families in your community.

Prayer

Begin planning your celebration with prayer. Set aside a time each day to seek the Lord's guidance as you organize the event. Ask a close friend to pray for you regularly during the weeks leading up to it. Meet and pray with your pastor.

Find a few prayer partners in your church who will commit to pray for the event from start to finish. Reproduce the *Prayer Checklist* on page 114 for them to use.

Put the program on your church's prayer list. If your church has a prayer chain, call and request prayer for training sessions, set-up time and the event itself.

Your party is a celebration of Jesus and an evangelistic outreach tool. Don't underestimate the importance of prayer for this event. "The prayer of a righteous man is powerful and effective" (James 5:16).

Setting a Date

The next step is to set a date. Do this as early as possible, and in consultation with your church's leadership. A conflict with another church group or event will limit your available space and drain your volunteer pool.

At many churches, an Easter festival works best on a Saturday morning during Lent. My favorite day is the Saturday before Palm Sunday, which is close enough to Easter to maximize impact, yet not an infringement on traditional Holy Week activities. An evening party is also a good choice because it accommodates working parents.

Limit your event to 2 hours if you anticipate hosting less than 150 children. For a larger group, plan a 2½ hour party so everyone has time to do all of the activities.

When reserving your church's facilities, be sure to secure the day before your program in addition to the actual time of your event. You will need the additional day to set up and decorate. See pages 24-31 for more information about set-up.

Volunteers

Recruiting helpers for this party is easy because it is a short, one-time commitment. Try to involve as many people as possible. In doing so, you will build excitement in your congregation.

Select activities (see page 14) and consult the sample *Schedule of Events* (see page 127) before you calculate your volunteer requirements. You will find that some helpers can manage two jobs when their responsibilities do not overlap. For example, volunteers at the registration table will have time to coordinate piñatas later on.

Some people might not be able to help during the party itself but are willing to lend a hand in other ways. Volunteers can cut out and prepare crafts, shop for supplies and assist with set-up and clean-up.

Recruiting. When you have a good idea of how many volunteers you will need, brainstorm a volunteer list using your church directory. Make a list of potential helpers. Choose those who like children, are fun to be around and are reliable. Don't forget to include teens and retirees!

Call those on your list, explain the program and ask them to be on your team. This is an important step. You want to build momentum and enthusiasm as soon as possible by developing a core group of helpers. In addition, people are more likely to commit time and energy if they are personally invited to be involved.

Duplicate the *Volunteer Sign-up Sheet* on page 115. Ask your first volunteers which jobs they would like to do and record their names on the sign-up sheet. Additional workers are more likely to help when they see that others are obligated already.

Use other means to recruit volunteers. Decorate your education area with colorful posters, such as those described on page 12. Put a notice in your church's bulletin and newsletter. Make an announcement during a church service. If your service is informal, pass around the sign-up sheet on a clipboard or post it on a table outside your sanctuary.

Ask for permission to visit adult and youth Sunday school classes, choir practices and other church groups that meet weekly. Explain the program, describe the jobs that are available and circulate your sign-up sheet.

Training. You may wish to schedule one large training session for all those participating. During that time you can explain in detail how the program will work and what each individual's responsibilities will be. An ideal opportunity to do this is at a designated hour during your set-up time.

Alternatively, you might need to better accommodate your helpers by offering individual or small group training. Some jobs are so simple that you can even train workers over the telephone! The *Volunteer Training Checklist* on page 116 will help you plan training sessions.

Budget

Create a list of supplies that you will need using the *Supply Checklist* on page 117. You may find you already have many of these items on hand. Determine what you must collect or purchase and estimate your expenses for the event. This total is your projected budget.

Find out if you can use any of your church's evangelism or outreach funds for the party. Perhaps your church's education department has some unallocated money to contribute to the event.

Reproduce the *Supply Donations Form* on page 118, fill in the necessary information and distribute it to your congregation in a bulletin insert or newsletter article. Ask members to contribute items on the list, making sure you specify a central collection point. Place a large laundry basket or decorated box in the collection location. Attach a sign that says, "Easter Party Supply Donations."

Ask if your church office can provide photocopying and postage for the event. This will reduce printing and postage expenses in your budget.

If possible, avoid charging visitors a registration fee. You are throwing a party to honor Jesus. Participants from your community are your guests – not your customers.

Publicity

In your congregation. Begin publicizing your event about six weeks in advance. Make sure it is described from the pulpit during announcements in your worship service. If this is your church's first Easter party, explain the purpose behind the celebration. Publish articles in your church bulletin and newsletter.

An Easter festival is an excellent first stepping-stone to evangelism. While many parishioners might be hesitant to invite a friend to a worship service, most feel comfortable telling a neighbor about a free Easter party for their children. Challenge your congregation to think of families they can invite.

Help your church members spread the word by providing a flyer in your church bulletin on the Sundays leading up to the event (or have a few children hand them to people as they leave the church service). The flyer should include the date, time and location of your program, as well as registration information. This will be a ready-made invitation that members can give to friends. Suggest they share it with neighbors, grandchildren, members of their child's soccer team, children at Boy Scouts and Girl Scouts or parents at PTA. A sample *Bulletin Insert* is on page 118.

Have a contest. Give church members a little incentive to recruit! Offer simple prizes, such as gift certificates to a fast-food restaurant, to the congregation members who have the most guests attend. This is a good way to involve children and youth in getting the word out.

In your community. Use the *Publicity Flyer* on page 119 to fill in your church's name, address and phone number as well as the date and time of your event. Or, ask a member of your congregation with computer skills to design a flyer using interesting fonts and clip art. Reproduce your flyer on brightly-colored paper.

Ask local businesses for permission to post your flyer in their windows. Make sure to inquire at day care centers, libraries and similar businesses that offer services important to young families. Some may allow you to leave a stack of flyers for their patrons to take. Check with nearby elementary schools for permission to send a flyer home with each child.

Order a banner from a local printer to put outside your church. This banner should be waterproof, colorful and tightly secured. It should include the date and time of your party, as well as a phone number for registration. While a banner is an added expense the first year you conduct an Easter program, it can be recycled each year if the printer uses replaceable plastic lettering for the date. Be sure to specify this when you order your banner.

Posters. Enlist a few volunteers to make posters to publicize the event in your church and community. Here are a few poster ideas to get you going:

"Fun at Easter? Egg-zactly" Poster

What You Need:

✓ egg pattern, page 120
✓ poster board or construction paper
✓ markers and crayons

What to Do:

1. Enlarge the egg pattern on poster board or construction paper (see page 19 for how to enlarge patterns).
2. Across the top of the poster, write, "Fun at Easter? Egg-zactly! Come to Easter Fun Day!"
3. Include necessary information inside the stripes of the egg.
4. Decorate the egg with bright markers and crayons.

Jesus Is Alive! Poster

What You Need:

✓ cross pattern, page 121
✓ poster board or construction paper
✓ markers

What to Do:

1. Enlarge the cross pattern on poster board or construction paper (see page 19 for how to enlarge patterns).
2. Across the top of the poster write, "Jesus Is Alive!"
3. Write "Celebrate at Easter Fun Day!" and the necessary information below the cross.
4. Decorate the outside of the cross with bright markers.

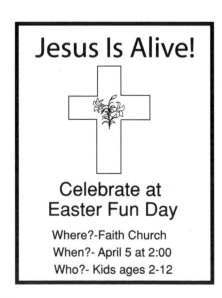

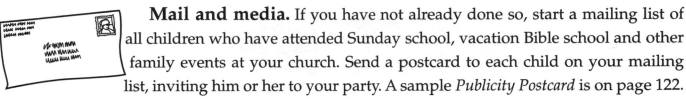

Mail and media. If you have not already done so, start a mailing list of all children who have attended Sunday school, vacation Bible school and other family events at your church. Send a postcard to each child on your mailing list, inviting him or her to your party. A sample *Publicity Postcard* is on page 122.

Place announcements in your local newspapers. Most publications have a community news or church events column that lists civic and church events for free.

Check with your local cable television station. Many will post local events on a "Community Calendar" at no charge.

Once your church sponsors a successful Easter celebration, word-of-mouth advertising will be a helpful ally in succeeding years as you reach out into your community.

Registration

Encourage pre-registration. If you know an approximate number of guests to expect for your party, you can plan appropriately to have enough craft supplies, prizes and eggs for the egg hunt.

Photocopy the *Registration Form* on page 122. Make sure that your church secretary has an ample supply to fill out when parents call to register by telephone.

Careful registration for this event will help you build your church's mailing list, so make sure to record each child's name, address and phone number. That way, children who attend your party can receive invitations to future church events such as vacation Bible school or Sunday School Kick-Off Day. Many who come to your celebration may not have a church home, so this is a wonderful opportunity to make them feel welcome at yours.

Be sure your registration form asks, "How did you hear about us?" This information will be important when you plan your next Easter party. You will learn from your participants which forms of publicity were the most effective.

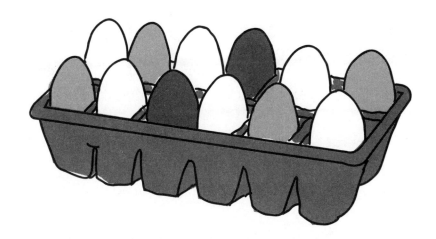

Planning

Selecting Activities

Each game, craft and snack presented here is designed to teach a point while having fun. All have a biblical basis. They can be used in any combination. Pick and choose activities that are appropriate for your situation.

Try to strike a good balance with your church's available space, volunteer pool and budget. When there are too few activity choices, children will get bored. However, if you offer too many options without adequate helpers and supplies, you may end up with chaos rather than celebration. Even small churches can put on a successful program with careful planning.

Solicit advice from the children's workers and Sunday school teachers in your church as you select activities. Your team may opt to organize a more focused party that centers on one theme, as outlined on pages 20-22.

Keep in mind that some children will spend a long time at one craft table, creating a masterpiece. Others will want to play a certain game several times. But in general, each game will take a child 3-5 minutes to play. Crafts require a bit more time — about 5-7 minutes per child. If you opt to include piñatas, an egg hunt and closing activities in your program, allocate at least 15 minutes for each.

Some games, such as *Carrot Toss* (page 36), *The Way to the Cross* (page 54) and *Who Betrayed Jesus?* (page 55) require more extensive preparation than others do. However, once you have made these game parts, you can use them year after year. Likewise, *Face Painting* (page 97), *Resurrection Eggs* (page 50) and *Beautiful Badges* (page 57) require more first-time expense, but you will find that investment in these tools was money well spent when you use them for your children's ministries every year.

Games & Prizes

As you choose games, be sure to include some for younger children (ages 3 through 6) as well as those that will challenge older ones (ages 7 through 12). Complete instructions for games begin on page 35.

Have at least one helper for each game. Games that call for two helpers can be streamlined to one if you are short on volunteers. Those designed for team play, such as *The Road Through Jerusalem* (page 53) and *Caterpillar Cocoon* (page 38) can be adapted for individuals by having children "race against the clock."

Helpers should become familiar with the game and play it a few times before your event begins. That way, they will know how long play will take for each child.

Volunteers should explain the rules to each child before play begins. Allow the children to play the games as many times as they wish, but encourage them to try all of the activities. If there are several children waiting to play one game, ask repeat players to move to the end of the line.

Games that require teams of children can be played as enough kids arrive at the booth to allow play. Or, consider scheduling a start time for relay games that allows all children to participate at once.

All children who play receive a prize. Have a prize box at each game station. The helper in charge of each game should distribute prizes.

Choose prizes that appeal to children, such as colorful stickers, washable tattoos, pencils, key chains, erasers and small toys. Many of these are available with Christian themes in novelty stores. Mail order companies also stock Christian novelties (see *Sources* on page 168).

Crafts

Crafts that symbolize new life, such as butterflies, flowers and crosses, provide an excellent opportunity to reinforce the message of Easter. The crafts outlined on pages 56-81 suit elementary school children. Toddlers and preschoolers will need adult assistance.

Have the craft helpers make sample crafts for their tables prior to the event. In doing so, they will discover what tricks to use, some pitfalls to avoid and how long the crafts will take to complete. The samples become models for participants to follow.

Provide at least one large table per craft because you likely will have several children working at each station at the same time. Allow each child to work at his or her own pace. Have extra supplies for children who want to make more than one of each craft item.

Remind volunteers to label each craft with the child's name.

Snacks

You may wish to have a group of volunteers prepare and serve a snack to your guests. Or you can supervise participating children as they make the snack themselves. Recipes and instructions for Easter snacks begin on page 82.

To guarantee that each child gets an opportunity to have a snack (and to thwart a few hungry youngsters from gobbling all the goodies early in your event), require tickets for the snack station. Reproduce the *Snack Tickets* on page 123 and distribute one to each guest at registration. Youngsters must surrender their snack ticket to a volunteer when they are ready to eat.

Have children wash their hands before and after they eat. Specify that children must consume their snack at the snack station to prevent a trail of crumbs throughout your facility.

Additional Activities

Balloon Hats. Many people are unfamiliar with balloon art, but it is easy to learn and kids love it. While no prior experience is necessary, volunteers at this station need to be willing to invest a few hours prior to your event to practice inflating the balloons and constructing the hats. Practice is important so the volunteer can make the hat while talking with the child.

From the instructions on pages 93-96, choose one or two hats that fit your program. High-quality pencil balloons and balloon pumps are available at party supply stores and through companies listed in *Sources*, page 168.

Face Painting. Volunteers at the face painting table need not be particularly creative. They can select a few patterns from page 165 and practice them before the event. Or, a helper with an artistic bent can create original designs. It takes several minutes to interact with each child, allow him or her to choose a pattern, and paint a design on the child's cheek or hand. For a large party, recruit more than one volunteer for this station. Face painting is popular with children — multiple helpers will prevent a long waiting line.

Find face paint at discount department stores and craft supply stores. Detailed face painting instructions are on page 97.

Petting Zoo. Invite a congregation member who owns small animals to bring his or her pets to the party. Or ask local pet shop owners to bring some of their rabbits to your event. More *Petting Zoo* instructions are on page 98.

Piñatas. Find inexpensive, colorful piñatas at discount department stores, dime stores and party supply shops. See *Sources* on page 168 if you cannot locate affordable piñatas in your area.

Fill piñatas with candies, prizes and stickers. Be sure that candies are wrapped since they likely will fall on the ground when the piñata breaks.

Separate children into age groups and move them to different parts of your campus to play. Recruit enough helpers so that all piñatas can be played simultaneously. Men are particularly good leaders for this event. Instructions for piñatas are on page 99.

The Easter Story. Pages 100-101 describe ways to present the Easter story. Choose a method that will use your resources wisely and give maximum impact. Because there will be very young children in your audience, limit the presentation to 10 minutes. Guests who have never heard the Gospel will be listening, so careful preparation for this segment is important!

One advantage of presenting the story at a single, scheduled time is that all participants — both kids and parents — will hear it. A good time to do this is during your closing activities. But if you think your closing will be too long, you might want to include the story as a station for smaller groups.

Once children have heard the story, distribute *Egg Hunt Tickets* (page 124). Since kids cannot take part in the hunt without a ticket, they will be sure to visit the story station or assembly.

Egg Hunt. The best way to conclude your celebration is with an Easter egg hunt. At your closing activities or final gathering, give children instructions for the hunt and collect their egg hunt tickets. Dismiss them by age groups to specified areas of your church grounds where the eggs have been hidden. Have at least one helper lead each group of children. Dismiss younger children first so they are not trampled in the rush. Additional instructions for a successful *Egg Hunt* are on page 102.

 # Closing Activities

A closing will ensure that all your guests will be together at one time. Participants can gather in one place, such as your sanctuary or fellowship hall. Stop all games, crafts and activities at this point.

Should your team decide to make a single presentation of the Easter story to the entire group, they can do so now. This is also a good time to announce winners of the *Jelly Bean Guessing Game* (page 46) and the *Coloring Contest* (page 40) and pass along instructions for the egg hunt.

You can lead your guests in some singing during this assembly. Choose simple songs such as "Jesus Loves Me," "This Little Light of Mine," "Jesus Loves the Little Children" or other easy praise choruses. You may wish to use an overhead projector or a handout to provide words since visitors may be unfamiliar with the music.

At the conclusion of the closing, invite visitors to worship with you on Sunday, calling their attention to the church ministry handout that they received at registration. Remind parents to fill out a *Visitor Evaluation Form* (see sample on page 125) before they leave.

 # The Easter Bunny

Should your church include the Easter Bunny in an evangelistic event? Discuss this issue with your team and pastor. An Easter Bunny can add to the festive atmosphere of your party. If he is unobtrusive, the Bunny will not detract from the focal point of the event: Jesus' resurrection. However, if you think the Bunny will divert attention from your message, don't include this element in your celebration.

If you decide to use the Easter Bunny, find a talented seamstress in your congregation to make a costume. Recruit an adult or mature teen to portray the Bunny. He can circulate among guests for about an hour. Since the Bunny does not speak, he will interact with the children in other ways. Give him a basket of lollipops or treats to distribute. Have him pat children on the head, wave or give older kids a "high five."

The Easter Bunny can be used as an effective follow-up tool when combined with photos. Have a volunteer take pictures of young visitors with the Bunny. The volunteer should record the names of those captured on film. A week or two afterward, mail each photo to the appropriate child with a note that says, "Thank you for coming to our party! We hope you can join us for Sunday school [Vacation Bible School, or any suitable event]."

See pages 33-34 for more follow-up ideas.

Your Pastor

An Easter party is an excellent opportunity for your pastor to meet people from the community who are not members of your congregation. Give your pastor the date of your event as soon as it is scheduled on the church calendar. Ask your pastor to attend the celebration not as a helper, but as host of the day.

Encourage your pastor to greet guests and introduce himself or herself. The pastor will want to invite those with no church home to worship with you. Your pastor may also wish to offer visitors pastoral care, such as hospital visitation, should a family need it.

Parents

Even though an Easter party is a program designed to reach children, their parents usually bring them. Because these adults are your guests as well, it is important to make them feel comfortable and welcome.

Set up a coffeepot in the snack area as a way of extending special hospitality to the parents. If possible, provide extra chairs throughout your facility, particularly near the games and crafts, to allow visiting adults to watch while their children participate.

Some parents enjoy helping their children with crafts and other activities. Encourage your volunteers to interact with the adults and the children.

Specify in your publicity that children younger than age 6 will need adult supervision. This will prevent your program from becoming a drop-off event. Also, the parents will provide extra hands to help in the preschoolers' game and craft areas as they assist their children.

Weather

Consider what to do with outdoor activities if the weather is unsuitable. Make sure to have a plan.

On the day of your event, evaluate the weather conditions. If there are only a few sprinkles, you can proceed with outdoor activities. Most children will come appropriately dressed for the few minutes they are outside.

In the case of a downpour or snowstorm, you will need to use your alternate plan. You may need to cancel the piñatas and egg hunt, the two activities most often held outdoors. Compensate by giving each child several colored Easter eggs at the conclusion of closing activities. Save the piñatas for next year's party.

Since most parents are grateful for an activity to occupy their children on a rainy day, few will complain if you must call off some portion of the event.

Make sure your prayer team asks the Lord for good weather for your celebration!

Enlarging Patterns

Some games and decorations have oversized parts which are easy to enlarge from patterns in this book.

What You Need:

✓ pattern to be enlarged
✓ overhead projector
✓ reusable overhead transparency
✓ transparency marker
✓ poster board or poster paper
✓ clear tape or push pins
✓ pencil
✓ permanent marker

What to Do:

1. Trace the pattern onto an overhead transparency using a transparency marker.
2. Attach poster board or poster paper to a wall. With overhead projector and transparency pattern, project the image onto the poster board or paper. Trace the pattern with a pencil, then reinforce the image with a permanent marker.

Creating Pattern Templates

Many activities require pattern templates, which are simple to make from the patterns in this book.

What You Need:

✓ pattern to be templated
✓ lightweight paper
✓ poster board
✓ pencil
✓ scissors
✓ clear, adhesive-backed plastic

What to Do:

1. Photocopy or trace the pattern onto paper. Cut out the pattern.
2. Trace the pattern onto poster board and cut it out.
3. If desired, cover the pattern with clear, adhesive-backed plastic for durability.

Party & Lesson Themes

You may want to plan your event around a single theme. Or, perhaps you are planning a small party with just a few activities. At other times you might need program ideas for Sunday school lessons, children's church or Bible clubs. The following list sorts the activities in this book according to events and topics related to Easter. Look for each theme's icon on activity pages throughout the book. These themes can give you ideas about what to include in your program, or simply make your planning easier!

Hosanna! (Palm Sunday)

In the Upper Room (The Last Supper)

At the Cross (The Crucifixion)

He is Alive! (The Resurrection)

Bunny Ears, page 59

Chick Pencil Topper, page 62

Cottontail Basket, page 65

Snacks: *Chick Cracker*, page 84

Rainbow Pretzels, page 90

Additional Activities: *Easy Bunny Ears*, page 94

Oversize Bunny Ears, page 96

It's Spring! (New Life in Christ)

Games: *Easter Bonnet Toss*, page 42

Springtime Limbo, page 52

Crafts: *Plastic Wrap Flower Stick*, page 76

Spring Flower Basket, page 79

Tissue Paper Flowers, page 80

Snack: *Orange Sunshines*, page 89

Additional Activity: *Bee Bonnet*, page 93

Planning Timetable

Use this Planning Timetable as you count down to your event.

4 months ahead

✓ Begin praying for your event

✓ Recruit prayer partners; give each one a *Prayer Checklist* (page 114)

✓ Set a date

✓ Reserve church facilities

2 months ahead

✓ Begin recruiting volunteers by telephone

✓ Start publicity within your congregation

✓ Make flyers, posters, bulletin inserts, publicity postcards and registration forms

✓ Order outside banner

✓ Select activities

✓ Organize a supply list

✓ Establish a budget

1 month ahead

✓ Put up flyers, posters and outside banner at your facility

✓ Put up flyers and posters at community businesses

✓ Submit announcements to local media

✓ Place bulletin inserts or announcements in worship bulletins each week until event

✓ Distribute supply list to congregation

✓ Set up supply collection point

✓ Begin collecting supplies and prizes

✓ Order litter bags to use as take-home bags

✓ Recruit volunteers from youth group, Sunday school classes and other groups

3 weeks ahead

✓ Mail publicity postcards

✓ Finish recruiting volunteers

✓ Schedule training sessions

✓ Construct needed game materials

✓ Reproduce necessary craft patterns

✓ Make decorations

✓ Assign volunteers to their tasks

2 weeks ahead

✓ Plan where you will set up each activity

✓ Finish collecting supplies and prizes

✓ Begin making sample crafts

1 day ahead

✓ Set up for the event (see *Set-up Checklist*, page 126)

Celebration Day

✓ Inflate balloons

✓ Hide Easter eggs

✓ Celebrate Jesus' resurrection!

Set-up

Set-up Time!

An Easter festival is an outreach event, but it also promotes fellowship among church members. This bonus is priceless to any congregation. Do all you can to foster it!

One way to cultivate fellowship is to involve as many helpers as possible in setting up for the program. As your team works together, excitement will build. Even adults look forward to a party! In addition, workers who help with set-up have a stake in the event. They want to see it succeed! Finally, by including a large group in preparation, you distribute the workload among many volunteers rather than a few, so your team will not be exhausted before even greeting the first guests.

Schedule a specific day and time for set-up. Put this information on your church calendar and in the church bulletin several weeks in advance. If your party is in the morning or afternoon, schedule set-up for the preceding day to give volunteers time to rest between set-up and the actual event. If the party is in the evening, plan to set up that morning. You will need the afternoon break before your visitors arrive.

Use the *Set-up Checklist* on page 126 to guide you. To maximize the use of your set-up time, have your plans and materials ready. List all of your activities and know where you will position each one. Take photos of your activity stations after they are assembled. These will be big helps in planning your event next year.

Set-up helpers can arrange tables and chairs, organize game stations, prepare and cut out craft parts, decorate your facility and stuff Easter eggs. This is also a good time to train volunteers for activity stations, prepare sample crafts, practice games and rehearse the Easter story. Don't forget to plan a time of prayer with your volunteers during set-up.

Prepare a *Beautiful Badge* (page 57) for each volunteer. Distribute these during set-up time or immediately before your party. Your team can wear their badges as a means of identifying themselves to your guests. Let them keep the badges afterward as a "thank you" for helping with the event.

A thorough set-up is important for the success of your program. Use it to take care of as many details as possible. You do not want to be searching for craft glue or tissue paper when guests arrive for your party!

Stations

Every activity you include needs its own station. Before you set up, decide where you will locate each one. Draw a map or chart for your team to use as they get ready.

A fellowship hall is ideal for game and craft stations. If you have a large, open room, you can arrange the station tables in long rows or a U-shape. This will encourage participants to proceed through the set-up methodically.

A group of classrooms also facilitates foot traffic. Children can move easily through the hallway from one station to the next.

Assess your remaining space. Consider using your outside grounds, extra classrooms, church kitchen and sanctuary. Smaller churches may need to be creative as they arrange stations.

If possible, set up several activities outdoors. This works well for the more physical games, such as basketball, relay races and piñatas. If a petting zoo is part of your program, find out if the animals should be kept inside or outside.

Locate your snack station either in the church kitchen or as close to it as possible. The refrigerator will be nearby for supplies and the sink will be handy for spills.

Position age-appropriate activities together. Parents of preschoolers will feel more comfortable if their little ones are set apart from the older children.

If you will be presenting the Easter story several times as an activity, do so in a quiet place away from the hustle and bustle. It will be easier for your audience to give complete attention to the presentation if they are not distracted.

Make sure each station has plenty of room. Allow one large table for each game or craft. Have a few chairs at each station for volunteers and visiting parents. Children can stand around the tables as they work.

Label each activity with a large piece of poster board, bright markers and *Sunshine Smiles* (page 29). Include each activity's Scripture reference on your posters. Have an extra table or area covered with newspapers for crafts that require drying time.

Registration Table

Set up a registration table at the front of your facility. Make sure this station is clearly marked. Children who have pre-registered will check in here. Walk-in guests can complete a registration form.

One way to ensure that you get all of the necessary registration information from each family is to position the *Jelly Bean Guessing Game* (page 46) at the registration table. Once a child registers or checks in, he or she may participate in the game.

At the registration table, families should receive a *Schedule of Events* (page 127), take-home bag, name tag and *Snack Ticket* for each child. Volunteers at this table should be prepared to direct guests to various activities and answer any questions they might have. If your facility is large or activities are spread out, include a simple map with the registration packet.

Ask your pastor for a handout that lists your church's weekly schedule and ministry opportunities. Make sure each visiting family receives a copy of this brochure.

Reproduce the *Visitor Evaluation Form* on page 125 and distribute it with pens to parents as they arrive. Have helpers explain that your church wants to meet families' needs in the best way possible, and that this completed form will help them do so. Volunteers can invite parents to fill out the form and place it in a labeled box near your exit as they leave.

Take-Home Bags

As children spend time at your party, they will accumulate crafts that they make and prizes they win from games. To prevent confusion, provide bags in which each child can collect his or her belongings.

You may elect to have each child make a bag. Helpers at the registration table can instruct children to make their first stop at the *Bunny Bag* station (page 58).

Pre-printed litter bags, such as the bags used in cars, are another option. Your church can order a large number of these bags to use at events in addition to this one. When ordered in quantity, litter bags are relatively inexpensive (printers are familiar with this process). Have the printer include your church's name, address, phone number and Sunday schedule on the outside of the bag.

Avoid mix-ups by writing each child's name on his or her bag.

Posted Schedule

Post a *Schedule of Events* that lists the times and locations of your activities. Have the schedule available at your registration area and throughout your facility. Since many children are eager to have the piñatas and egg hunt right away, specify the times of these events. Make sure your helpers know the timetable so they can answer any questions from visitors. A sample is on page 127.

Traffic Flow

Make a poster showing a simple layout of your facility to hang at the entrance. Place posters with arrows at strategic points. For example, make a sign that says, "Crafts Downstairs," with an arrow pointing downward, and place it at the top of your stairwell.

Plan to guide children to activities that have short waiting lines. If a volunteer finds his or her line getting too long, the volunteer might say to a few children, "Why don't you go make a *Resurrection Rainbow*? By the time you are finished, there will be room here for you."

 # Decorations

Decorate your facility with symbols of spring and new life: flowers, crosses, butterflies, eggs, sunshine faces, baskets, palm branches, lambs, rabbits and chicks. Pastels are popular during this time of year. Or, use bright colors to create a carnival atmosphere.

If your church has an outdoor Easter display, such as a cross draped with purple fabric, ask those in charge of it to set it up prior to your event.

Balloons and crepe paper streamers must be put up just before your party so they will still have their fresh lift. Other decorations can be prepared a few weeks in advance. Invite your church's youth group, women's group, senior citizens group and Sunday school classes to participate in party preparation by making some of these simple decorations.

Butterfly Mosaics

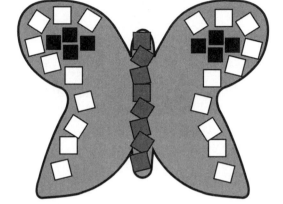

What You Need:

✓ *Butterfly Mosaic* pattern, page 128
✓ construction paper in various colors
✓ craft glue
✓ scissors

What to Do:

1. Duplicate the Butterfly Mosaic pattern on construction paper.
2. Cut out the butterfly.
3. Select other paper in contrasting colors. Cut or rip the paper into ½" squares.
4. Decorate butterfly wings and body using glue and ½" squares.

Eggs-traordinary Eggs

Sponsor a coloring contest for your Sunday school kids or young teens. Have each contestant color an *Eggs-traordinary Egg* as an entry. Award simple prizes to all participants. Not only will they all have fun, they will also be pleased to help with party preparation. And you will have decorations for your event!

What You Need:

✓ egg pattern, page 120
✓ white poster board or construction paper
✓ scissors
✓ markers or crayons
✓ prizes

What to Do:

1. Reproduce the egg pattern onto poster board or construction paper.
2. Color the eggs with markers or crayons or use the plain pattern in a coloring contest.
3. Cut out the eggs.

Flowered Crosses

Many churches display flower-decked crosses, similar to these, on Easter morning.

What You Need:

✓ cross pattern, page 121
✓ white poster board or large piece of cardboard
✓ colored tissue paper
✓ ruler
✓ scissors
✓ craft glue

What to Do:

1. Enlarge the cross pattern on poster board or a large piece of cardboard. (See page 19 for how to enlarge patterns.) Cut out the cross.
2. Cut tissue paper into 6" squares.
3. Crumple each square into a cluster. Glue the clusters onto the cross.
4. Make sure the cross is covered with tissue. Allow the cross to dry before hanging.

Spring Vines

What You Need:

✓ green raffia
✓ instructions and materials for *Tissue Paper Flowers*, page 80
✓ crepe paper streamers (optional)
✓ clear tape

What to Do:

1. To create vines, cut or tie green raffia into 5-6' lengths.
2. Make six *Tissue Paper Flowers* for every 5-6' raffia vine.
3. Attach the *Tissue Paper Flowers* to the vine by twisting chenille wire stems around the raffia. Space the flowers every 12-15" inches along the vine.
4. If desired, wind crepe paper streamers around the vines for a festive effect.
5. Drape *Spring Vines* in doorways or along table edges and secure with clear tape.

Sunshine Smiles

There are at least three ways to create these cheery faces.

Method #1: Copy and Trace

What You Need:

✓ *Sunshine Smiles* pattern, page 129
✓ poster board
✓ yellow poster board or construction paper
✓ pencil
✓ black marker
✓ scissors

What to Do:

1. Make a template from the *Sunshine Smiles* pattern. (See page 19 for how to make a pattern template.)
2. With the template, trace the pattern onto yellow poster board or construction paper.
3. Trace over the pencil markings with a black marker.
4. Cut out the *Sunshine Smiles*. Copy the facial markings with a pencil and reinforce them with black marker.

Method #2: Photocopying

What You Need:

✓ *Sunshine Smiles* pattern, page 129
✓ yellow paper
✓ photocopy machine
✓ scissors

What to Do:

1. Load the yellow paper into the photocopy machine following the manufacturer's instructions.
2. Use the pattern to reproduce *Sunshine Smiles* on yellow paper.
3. Cut out the *Sunshine Smiles*.

Method #3: Enlarging with Overhead Projector

What You Need:

✓ large piece of yellow poster board, 20" x 28"
✓ overhead projector
✓ reusable overhead transparency
✓ transparency marker
✓ *Sunshine Smiles* pattern, page 129
✓ black permanent marker
✓ scissors

What to Do:

1. Enlarge the *Sunshine Smiles* pattern on poster board. (See page 19 for how to enlarge patterns.)
2. Cut out the *Sunshine Smiles*.

Crepe Paper Cascades

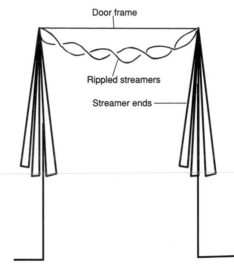

What You Need:

✓ rolls of crepe paper streamers in assorted colors
✓ clear tape
✓ scissors
✓ step stool or ladder

What to Do:

1. With clear tape, secure the end of one streamer to the ceiling where it meets the corner and the wall.
2. Unravel the streamer to the center of the room.
3. Twist the streamer for a ripple effect.
4. Tape the streamer to the ceiling at the center of the room. Cut the streamer about two or three feet below this taped position.
5. Repeat these steps for streamers, beginning in each corner of the room and at periodic intervals along the walls.

Note: Take extra care with your balance as you tape streamers to the walls and ceiling.

Crepe Paper Arches

What You Need:

✓ rolls of crepe paper streamers in assorted colors
✓ yardstick or tape measure
✓ clear tape
✓ scissors
✓ step stool or ladder

What to Do:

1. With the tape measure or yardstick, measure the width of the doorway you want to decorate.
2. Double that figure. Measure and cut two or more contrasting crepe paper streamers to that length.
3. Layer the cut streamers and treat the stack as one.
4. Find the center of the streamers and position this point at the middle of the doorway's top frame.
5. Let the streamers loop down slightly below the top of the door frame, creating an arch. Twist the streamers for a ripple effect and tape them to the corners of the door frame.
6. Allow the remaining ends to hang down along the door frame.

Note: Take extra care with your balance as you tape streamers to the walls and ceiling.

 # Balloons

Because balloons lose their buoyancy in a few hours, you must inflate them just before your event. They will be one of the final touches you add to your celebration.

Helium balloons stay aloft, are versatile in decorating and are easier to inflate than regular balloons. Regular balloons are less expensive and free to inflate.

If renting a helium tank fits in your budget, select good-quality balloons (usually labeled "helium quality") to avoid breakage during inflation. Because string tends to tangle, use curling ribbon to anchor the balloons instead. Five- to six-foot lengths of ribbon can be cut in advance.

Whether you select helium or regular balloons, have an assembly-line team of volunteers ready to inflate and tie them. Secure bunches of balloons at your entrance, corners of rooms and at large stations. Use single balloons or pairs on the backs of chairs and around table legs.

If your budget allows, consider ordering bunches of pre-inflated helium balloons from a gift store or florist. Many businesses will deliver these just in time for your event.

Ask a few volunteers to gather all the balloons before the conclusion of the party. Have them distribute the balloons to children as they leave.

Balloon Arches and Pillars

One way to create a dramatic effect at an entrance or station is with balloon arches and pillars.

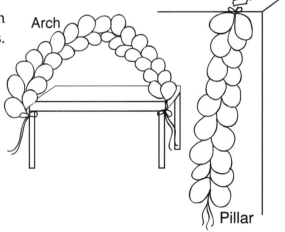

What You Need:

✓ inflated balloons
✓ curling ribbon
✓ measuring tape
✓ scissors
✓ clear tape

What to Do:

1. Measure the desired length of your arch or pillar. Add two feet (24") to that figure to allow you to secure the completed arch or pillar. Cut a piece of curling ribbon to the total length to make the "backbone" of the arch or pillar.
2. Tie a 6-8" piece of curling ribbon onto each inflated balloon.
3. Tie inflated balloons to the backbone as close together as possible. Trim excess ribbon close to the backbone.
4. If you are using helium balloons, create an arch by securing each end of the backbone to the floor, a piece of furniture or a handrail. The helium will cause the balloons to "arch" upward.
5. If you are using regular balloons, create a hanging pillar by securing one end of the backbone to the wall or ceiling. Balloons will then cascade down.
Note: If you plan a long arch or pillar, or you are contending with windy weather, use a double backbone.

After the Celebration

As Children Leave

Have volunteers posted at your exits to say good-bye to participants. If you included balloons or other giveaways in your program, this is the appropriate time to distribute them.

Remind departing parents to complete the *Visitor Evaluation Form* on page 125. Provide pencils and extra forms to those who need them. Have a labeled collection box near your exit.

Thank each family for coming to your celebration. "We are so glad you joined us," "Please visit again" and "Happy Easter" are all good expressions for your helpers to use as guests leave.

Clean-up

Have your clean-up crew collect craft samples, remaining craft supplies, reusable decorations and game parts. Organize these leftovers in large plastic storage bins or cardboard boxes. Tape a detailed contents list on the outside of each box and store the boxes in a safe place for use next year.

Program Evaluation

Staff Evaluation. Feedback from volunteers is essential for effective ministry. Give each helper a *Volunteer Evaluation Form* (page 125). Place a box for completed forms near your exit. Ask your team to complete the form before leaving.

Visitor Evaluation. Review what your guests shared about your program on their evaluation forms. Pass along positive comments to your volunteers when you thank them for their participation.

Easter party file. Start an Easter party file. Make a list of crafts, games, snacks and activities that you included in your program. Note the number of supplies you purchased.

Next to each activity, record feedback. Information from completed evaluation forms will help you assess each activity. Which crafts and games were more popular than others? Did you have enough materials? Store photos of your activity stations with these comments.

Make a note on your calendar to scour after-Easter sales for decorations that you can use next year. Store them with leftover craft supplies, samples and game parts.

Write notes on other aspects of your program. Did following a planning timetable help you? Include a copy of your preparation procedure.

Who were your volunteers? Were they adequately trained? Keep a list of names so that you will know whom to ask to help you next year.

Include samples of publicity and bulletin flyers, a blank registration form and a publicity postcard in your file. Record the number who attended. From the returned *Visitor Evaluation Forms* and *Registration Forms*, take careful note of how participants found out about your program. Determine which kinds of publicity were most effective.

What were weather conditions on the day of your event? Did this alter your plans? Did your backup scenario work?

Jot down ideas while they are still fresh. Your file will help you be better organized for next year. It will also enable you to produce a higher-quality event the second time around because you will know what worked well and what you need to change.

Thank-you's. Send a thank-you note to each of your volunteers. Let them know you appreciated their help and that you look forward to working with them again.

Then, sit down, munch some leftover jellybeans and praise God for the opportunity to share the Good News of an empty tomb with the children and families of your community!

Follow-up

The weeks of prayer and preparation are past. Balloons have popped. Plastic grass has been vacuumed away. But your Easter party is not over. For some children and families, your event can mark the beginning of a new life. Take advantage of the opportunity you have to reach out to those who joined you for your celebration.

Mailing lists. Enlist your church secretary and church office facilities to help you create mailing lists from the completed registration forms. If your church office uses a computer, be sure to get a hard copy as well as a disk copy of each mailing list to preserve registration information in the event of computer malfunction.

The first mailing list, "Participating Children," should include the names and addresses of all children who came to your event. Shortly after your party, mail a postcard or letter to all of the children on this list. Thank them for coming to your celebration and invite them to the next children's event at your church (such as vacation Bible school). If you took children's pictures with the Easter Bunny, send each child's photo with this letter.

Create a second mailing list, "Non-member Families," by extracting the names and addresses of families who do not attend your church. Write a follow-up letter directed to those families. Use the *Follow-up Letter* on page 127 as a model, or reproduce it and fill in the appropriate information about your church. You (or the party coordinator if it was someone else) and your pastor should both sign a copy of the letter for each non-member family. Mail these letters immediately after your event.

If a mailing list is new to your children's ministries, continue to keep careful registration records at future children's and family events. Ask your pastor to pass along the names and addresses of families who visit your church for worship. Use this new information to build your list. Update it at least once a year.

From registration information, keep track of children's birthdays. When youngsters reach their teens, their names can be transferred to your church's youth group mailing list.

Home and Telephone Visits. Ask friendly, outgoing people to visit non-member families who came to the event. If your church has a visitation or evangelism committee, find out if they can help. Emphasize to members that they should make a courtesy call to families before visiting rather than just "dropping by."

Some people may be intimidated at the thought of visiting a stranger on behalf of their church. If so, remind them that the purpose of their visit is to simply thank families for coming to your event. As a gesture of love and caring, members may wish to take along a small gift, such as a potted flower, a jar of *Upper Room Snack Mix* (page 91) or a plate of *Lamb Cookies* (page 88).

During visits, members should thank families for coming to your party, ask if they have any needs that your church can meet and invite them to worship on Easter Sunday. Conversation starters could include: "Did your children have a good time?" "What did they like best?" "How long have you lived in the community?" "How did you hear about us?" "Have you been to an event at our church before?" Members can also pass along a copy of your church's brochure that lists ministries, phone numbers and other information.

Afterward, ask your team about their visits. Non-member families might have shared personal needs that your church and pastor will want to address. You may also get reaction to your program that might not have been reported on an evaluation form.

Today, many people complain about the frenetic pace of life. A personal visit to a home takes time and initiative. It speaks volumes to non-members about your church's love and concern. Make every effort to arrange home visits to non-member families.

Perhaps there are only a couple of days between your party and Holy Week services at your church. If so, have volunteers telephone visitors immediately after the party to invite them to Easter Sunday worship. They can follow up with a home visit a week or two later.

In your congregation. Communicate the successes of your event to your congregation. Publicly thank those who participated. Submit a brief report to the church's newsletter and weekly bulletin. Share a testimony during worship. Convey appreciation to your prayer partners and prayer chain for their ministry.

In short, "Give thanks to the Lord… make known among the nations what he has done" (Psalm 105:1).

Games

Carrot Toss Ages 3-12

Bible Reference: Consider the lilies, Luke 12:27-28

Overview

As children toss beanbag carrots to the bunny, they will learn that God provides for all of their needs.

Helpers: 2

- 1 person to hand out beanbags and distribute prizes
- 1 person to retrieve beanbags

Materials

- ❏ 20" x 28" piece of white poster board
- ❏ 20" x 28" piece of plywood
- ❏ 2" x 24" piece of plywood
- ❏ 3" hinge and screws
- ❏ eyelet screw
- ❏ electric jigsaw
- ❏ electric drill
- ❏ 18" medium-weight string
- ❏ *Bunny Parts* patterns, page 130
- ❏ compass and pencil
- ❏ black permanent marker
- ❏ clear, adhesive-backed plastic
- ❏ craft glue
- ❏ orange and green felt
- ❏ *Carrot Beanbag* pattern, page 131
- ❏ needle and thread or sewing machine
- ❏ uncooked popcorn kernels, rice or dry beans
- ❏ rubber bands
- ❏ scissors
- ❏ masking tape

Preparation

1. Use the compass and pencil to draw a 9" circle and a 10" circle below it on poster board. This is the bunny body.
2. Duplicate and cut out the bunny parts. Trace the parts on the bunny body in the appropriate places. Reinforce the bunny outline with a permanent marker.
3. Cut out the center of the larger circle, which will be the bunny's tummy.
4. Cover the entire poster board with clear, adhesive-backed plastic.
5. Lay the poster board over the 20" x 28" piece of plywood. Trace the opening for the bunny's tummy onto the plywood. Cut out the opening with a jigsaw.
6. Attach a hinge and the 2" x 24" piece of plywood to the center back of the bunny board to create an easel. Attach an eyelet screw to the inside bottom center of the bunny board.
7. With a drill, make a small hole in the bottom of the easel board. Tie one end of the string through the eyelet screw and one end through the easel hole.
8. Glue the poster board onto the front of the plywood bunny board.
9. Reproduce the *Carrot Beanbag* patterns. Trace and cut out three carrots from

front view

back view

orange felt and three carrot tops from green felt.

10. With a needle and thread or a sewing machine, attach the green carrot top to the top edge of the orange carrot. Then sew the sides of the carrot together, beginning at the carrot's top seam and continuing down to the tip. Do not sew the edges of the green carrot tops together.

11. Repeat for the remaining two carrots.

12. Fill the carrots with popcorn kernels, rice or dried beans. Secure the top with a rubber band. Cut fringe in the green felt to look like carrot tops.

13. Set up the bunny on a table or desk in your play area. With masking tape, mark two throwing lines: one closer for younger children and one farther back for older children.

Note: While this game takes extra preparation the first time, the bunny and *Carrot Beanbags* are very durable and can be used from year to year.

How to Play

1. Line up the children behind a masking tape line. Say, **The bunny is hungry. Can you feed him some carrots?**

2. Each child should try to toss the carrots into the bunny's tummy. All the children receive a prize.

3. Say, **Just like you are feeding the bunny, God feeds us and provides for all of our needs.**

Caterpillar Cocoon Ages 3-12

Bible Reference: Jesus is buried in the tomb, Matthew 27:57-60

Overview

The butterfly, a symbol of the resurrection, starts off as a caterpillar in a cocoon. Likewise, Jesus was wrapped in cloth, put in the tomb and broke free on Easter morning. In this game, children will break free of their cocoons, just like butterflies — and Jesus — do.

Helpers: 1

- one person to explain the rules and coach the teams as they wrap their cocoons

Materials

- ❑ toilet tissue
- ❑ prizes

Preparation

You will need at least four children to conduct this game. Have one roll of toilet tissue for each child.

How to Play

1. Divide the children into two teams. Teams can have mixed ages.

2. Ask, **How does a caterpillar become a butterfly?** Allow the children to respond. Then say, **Yes, the caterpillar wraps himself in a cocoon and later emerges as a butterfly.**

3. Have the children select one person on each team to become the "cocoon." Remind them that a smaller person is faster to wrap than a larger person!

4. Instruct the "cocoons" to stand straight and still.

5. Give each wrapper a roll of toilet tissue. Caution them that the tissue breaks easily if it is pulled too tightly or too quickly. If the tissue breaks, the children should keep working.

6. At your signal, the teams should begin "wrapping" their cocoons. All wrappers on each team can work simultaneously to cover the cocoon. The team that finishes first is the winner. All participants receive a prize.

7. Say, **Butterflies, break free!** Children in the cocoons should break out of the tissue and begin to fly. Say, **(Child's name) and (Child's name) broke free of their cocoons, just like butterflies do. After His death on the cross, Jesus was wrapped in linen cloth and put in a grave. But He broke free on Easter morning!**

Clean Pennies Ages 3-12

Bible Reference: Jesus cleanses hearts, Revelation 21:5

Overview

Jesus said, "I am making everything new!" Children will make a dirty penny clean and learn that Jesus can do the same for them.

Helpers: 1

- one person to assist the children with the pennies

Materials

- ❑ pennies
- ❑ small bowls
- ❑ spoons
- ❑ vinegar
- ❑ salt
- ❑ measuring cup
- ❑ measuring spoon
- ❑ soft cloths

Preparation

Select pennies that are more than 12 years old (older than the children participating). Choose pennies that are as dark as possible. Avoid bright, shiny pennies.

How to Play

1. Measure ¼ cup vinegar and ½ teaspoon salt in each bowl. Mix together.

2. Invite each child to select a penny. Point out that the pennies are older than any child present.
3. Ask each child to carefully drop a penny into a bowl. Allow only one penny per bowl at a time.
4. Have the children watch the pennies for about 20 seconds to see how they change color.
5. Let the children remove the pennies from the bowls with spoons. They can use soft cloths to dry and buff the pennies.
6. Say, **Did you notice that all of these pennies were old and dirty yet they still became clean? Jesus can do the same with us. When we ask for His help, He can make us clean on the inside.**
7. Invite the children to take their pennies with them as a reminder that Jesus makes all things new. This games works well when coupled with *Love Banks* on page 72.

Coloring Contest Ages 3-12

Bible Reference: We are God's workmanship, Ephesians 2:10

Overview

The children will color Easter symbols and receive prizes for their workmanship

Helpers: 3

- one person to assist children as they color
- two people to award ribbons

Materials

- ❑ egg, cross and butterfly patterns on pages 133-135
- ❑ markers or crayons
- ❑ pencils
- ❑ miniature muffin pan liners, 2" diameter
- ❑ ½" or ¾" wide ribbon
- ❑ ruler
- ❑ *Coloring Contest Ribbon Centers*, page 132
- ❑ colorful paper
- ❑ stapler
- ❑ craft glue
- ❑ clear tape or paper clips

Preparation

1. Choose a cross, butterfly or Easter egg design for the contest. Duplicate one for each child.
2. Cut one 15" length of ribbon for each child's award. Loop each ribbon and staple it to the back of a miniature muffin liner. Cut a fringe on the edges of the liner paper.
3. Reproduce the *Ribbon Centers* on colorful paper. Cut out each center. Glue one center to the middle of each muffin liner. Make one award ribbon for each child (every participating child should receive an award).

How to Play

1. Give each child a design to color.
2. Provide crayons or markers. Help the children write their names and ages on the backs of their papers with pencils.
3. Have the children color their designs. Encourage them to do careful, creative work.
4. Say, **You are doing such fine handiwork! The Bible says that God is creative, too. We are His workmanship. That means He took special care making each of us, just like you are taking special care in coloring your cross (or butterfly or egg).**
5. When all of the children are finished, sort and display the entries by age. Attach an award ribbon to each entry with clear tape or paper clips.

MOST COLORFUL

Cotton Ball Relay Ages 3-12

Bible Reference: Perseverance, Hebrews 12:1-3

Overview

Jesus modeled perseverance when He went to the cross. Children will see the importance of "running the race of perseverance" as they play this relay.

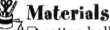

Helpers: 2

- one person to give instructions and referee the relay
- one person to distribute supplies and prizes

Materials

- ❑ cotton balls
- ❑ spoons
- ❑ masking tape or chalk
- ❑ two Easter baskets
- ❑ prizes

Preparation

1. Mark a starting line on the floor with masking tape or chalk.
2. Use masking tape or chalk to designate "race lanes" for each team.
3. Place the Easter baskets at the far end of the play area. The baskets will be the "cones" the children circle as they run back and forth in their lanes.

How to Play

1. Divide the children into two teams. Have them line up behind the starting line.
2. Give a spoon to each child.
3. Give a cotton ball to the first child in each line. Have them place cotton balls on spoons. Explain that the cotton ball must stay on the spoon.
4. Signal for the game to begin. The children must hold the spoon out in front of them as they run down the lane, circle the Easter basket, return to the starting line and place the cotton ball on the next player's spoon. If the cotton ball falls during play, they must stop and pick it up with the spoon.
5. Say, **Jesus persevered for us on the cross. Now run this race with perseverance!**
6. Distribute prizes to both the winning and losing teams for persevering until the end.

41

Easter Bonnet Toss Ages 3-12

Bible Reference: Christian clothing, Colossians 3:12

Overview

This game is a reminder that Christians clothe themselves with compassion, kindness, humility, gentleness and patience. Children will toss the bonnets onto a Maypole.

Helpers: 1

- one person to distribute bonnets, retrieve bonnets and hand out prizes

Materials

- ☐ piece of plywood, 12" x 12"
- ☐ electric drill
- ☐ ½" wide dowel, 12" long
- ☐ wood glue
- ☐ white paint
- ☐ paintbrush
- ☐ satin pastel ribbons
- ☐ scissors
- ☐ craft glue
- ☐ three toddler-size Easter bonnets or craft bonnets
- ☐ masking tape
- ☐ prizes

Preparation

1. Drill a hole in the center of the plywood. Glue the dowel in hole. When the glue is dry, use white paint to paint the assembly.

2. Cut two or three 18" length ribbons. With craft glue, secure one end of each ribbon to the top of the dowel. Twist the ribbons around the dowel for a maypole effect. Glue the ends of the ribbons near the bottom of the dowel and to the plywood top to secure.

3. In your play area, use masking tape to mark two tossing lines: one closer to the maypole for younger children, and one farther away for older children.

How to Play

1. Have a child stand behind the tossing line. Give the child three bonnets. Say, **Many people enjoy wearing special clothes, like these bonnets, on Easter. The Bible says that Christians have special clothes they can wear all the time: compassion, kindness, humility, gentleness and patience.**

2. Ask, **Can you toss the Easter bonnets onto the maypole?**

3. Each child receives a prize.

Easter Match-it Ages 3-12

Bible Reference: *The Easter story, John 12-20*

Overview

The children will match cards to review the Easter story.

 Helpers: 1

- one person to mix up the cards, discuss each symbol's importance and award prizes

 Materials

- ❑ *Easter Match-it Cards* patterns, page 136
- ❑ crayons or markers
- ❑ scissors
- ❑ clear, adhesive-backed plastic
- ❑ prizes

 Preparation

1. Reproduce two copies of the *Easter Match-it Cards* for each game set you want to make.
2. With crayons or markers, color the symbols on the cards. Be sure that both symbols on each page are colored identically.
3. Cut out the cards and cover them with clear, adhesive-backed plastic for durability.

 How to Play

1. Randomly arrange the cards face down on the table or floor. For younger children, use only two or three pairs. Older children will like the challenge of more cards to match.

2. The children should take turns turning over two cards at a time. Encourage them to remember where each symbol is located in the arrangement.

3. When a child makes a match, ask, **What is significant about this symbol?** If the child struggles for an answer, help with a brief review.

- Palm branch: Crowds used these to worship Jesus (John 12:13).
- Donkey: Jesus rode on a donkey into Jerusalem (John 12:14-15).
- Money bag: Judas betrayed Jesus for 30 pieces of silver (Matthew 26:14-15).
- Bread and cup: Jesus served these at the Last Supper with His disciples (Matthew 26:26-28).
- Rope: Guards bound Jesus with a rope (John 18:12).
- Cross: Jesus died on the cross (John 19).
- Angel: Angels announced Jesus' resurrection (John 20:11-12).
- Empty Tomb: Jesus is alive! (John 20:1-18).

4. When the children have uncovered all of the cards, award prizes.

Find the Empty Tomb Ages 3-12

Bible Reference: *The empty tomb, Luke 24:6*

Overview

In this game, children will look for Jesus' tomb. When they find it, they will learn that it is empty and He has risen.

Helpers: 2

- one person to help children with the "tombs"
- one person to help children decipher the messages from the empty tomb

Materials

- ❏ cereal bowls
- ❏ 2-3"-high plastic toy people
- ❏ *Empty Tomb* pattern, page 137
- ❏ 8½" x 11" white paper
- ❏ white crayons
- ❏ rubber bands
- ❏ watercolor paints
- ❏ paintbrushes
- ❏ newspapers
- ❏ smocks (men's old shirts work well)

Preparation

1. Duplicate the *Empty Tomb Scroll* pattern.
2. Cut the white paper into fourths so that each piece measures 4¼" x 5½". You will need one 4¼" x 5½" piece for each child.
3. Use a white crayon to trace the message from the Empty Tomb Scroll pattern onto each 4¼" x 5½" piece of paper.
4. Roll each scroll and secure with a rubber band.
5. Set up a "message deciphering area" away from the play area with newspapers, watercolors and paintbrushes.

How to Play

1. To create "tombs," turn cereal bowls upside down on a table or other flat surface. Use two or three tombs for younger children. Challenge older children by adding more tombs when they play the game.
2. Hide a plastic toy person under all but one tomb. Hide a prepared scroll under the empty tomb.
3. Mix the tombs by scooting them around with the items still under them. Allow one child to play at a time. Say, **Jesus was buried in one of the tombs. Can you find which one is Jesus' tomb?**
4. If a child opens a tomb and discovers a plastic toy person there, say, **No, that is not Jesus' tomb. Try again.**
5. When the child finds the tomb with the scroll, say, **There is no body in this tomb. But look, there is a message here for you.**
6. Have the child take his or her scroll to the message deciphering area. Help the child into an art smock to protect his or her clothing. Let the child use watercolors to paint across the scroll. The crayoned message will bleed through the watercolors.
7. Say, **The message is appearing! What does it say?** If the child can read, allow him or her to respond. Help younger ones read the message. **It says, "He is not here; He has risen." Jesus is alive!**
8. Give the child the scroll to take home as a reminder of Jesus' resurrection.

Garden Bowling Ages 3-12

Bible Reference: *In the Garden of Gethsemane, Mark 14:32-36*

Overview

Children know that gardens are planted in the spring. This game explains to children why one garden in particular — the Garden of Gethsemane — was so important in the Easter story.

Helpers: 2

- one person to reset the "bowling pins" and to roll balls back to the start line
- one person to encourage children and hand out prizes

Materials

- ❑ six 2-liter plastic soda bottles
- ❑ three small balls, such as tennis balls
- ❑ orange and green felt
- ❑ carrot pattern, page 138
- ❑ poster board
- ❑ hot glue gun
- ❑ scissors
- ❑ masking tape
- ❑ prizes

Preparation

1. Wash out the soda bottles and remove the labels. Allow the bottles to dry thoroughly.
2. Make a template of the carrot pattern. (See page 19 for how to make templates).
3. Use the template to cut six carrots from orange felt and six carrot tops from green felt.
4. With a hot glue gun, glue the carrots and carrot tops to the soda bottles, creating six "bowling pins."
5. Set up the bowling pins in a triangle at the end of your "alley." A long hallway makes an ideal alley.
6. With masking tape, mark two starting lines: one for older children, about 15-18 feet from the pins, and one for younger children, about 10 feet from the pins.

How to Play

1. Have the child stand behind the appropriate line. Give him or her three balls. Explain that it is time to pick the early crops from the spring garden. Tell the child to knock down as many carrots as possible to ensure a good spring harvest.
2. Say, **Spring is the perfect time to plant a garden. Jesus spent a lot of time in a garden the night before He went to the cross. He prayed and talked with God in the Garden of Gethsemane.**
3. Each child receives a prize.

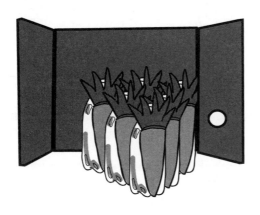

Jelly Bean Guessing Game
Ages 3-12

Bible Reference: God's omnipotence, Matthew 10:30

Overview

The children will guess the number of jelly beans in the bottle, and learn that God never has to guess at a number.

Helpers: 1

• one person to record the guesses

Materials

❑ 1- or 2-liter plastic soda bottle
❑ jelly beans
❑ 4-5" foam ball
❑ two 20-22mm wiggle eyes
❑ 1" pink pompon
❑ three pink chenille wires
❑ one cotton ball
❑ 30" colorful ribbon, 1" wide
❑ *Jelly Bean Rabbit* pattern, page 139
❑ poster board
❑ white and pink craft foam
❑ hot glue gun
❑ glue sticks
❑ craft glue
❑ scissors
❑ pencil
❑ envelope
❑ paper

Preparation

1. Wash the plastic soda bottle and remove its label. Allow the bottle to dry thoroughly.
2. Make a template of the *Jelly Bean Rabbit* pattern. (See page 19 for how to make pattern templates.)
3. Trace and cut two bunny ears, two hands and two paws from white craft foam.
4. Trace and cut two inner ears, six fingers and six toes from pink craft foam.
5. With craft glue, attach the inner ears to the outer ears, fingers to hands, and toes to paws.
6. Position and glue the eyes, pompom nose and chenille wire whiskers to the foam ball head.
7. With a hot glue gun, attach the ears to the back of the head, the hands around the sides of the soda bottle body, paws to the bottom of the body and a cotton ball tail to the back.
8. Count the jelly beans and pour them into the bottle. Record the total and seal the answer inside an envelope.
9. With a scissors tip, carve a hole in the bottom of the foam ball. Attach the ball to the top of the bottle.
10. Tie the ribbon in a bow around the neck of the bottle.

How to Play

1. Record each child's name and numerical guess.
2. When all children are finished guessing, open the envelope. Determine which child made the closest guess.
3. Say, **We could only guess at the number of jelly beans in the bunny. But God never has to guess. He even knows the number of hairs on our heads!**
4. Present the bottle of jelly beans to the winning child.

46

J-E-S-U-S Basketball Ages 5-12

Bible Reference: The Name above all names, Philippians 2:9-11

Overview

In a variation of "H-O-R-S-E," children will shoot baskets to spell "J-E-S-U-S," the name above all names.

Helpers: 2

- one to toss the ball back to the children
- one to keep track of the score and distribute prizes

Materials

- ❑ adjustable-height basketball hoop or a large trash can
- ❑ basketball
- ❑ masking tape or chalk
- ❑ prizes

Preparation

1. Set up the basketball hoop in a safe area. Because you will raise the hoop for older children and lower it for younger ones, practice adjusting the height several times. If you don't have a hoop, use a large trash can instead.
2. With masking tape or chalk, mark two shooting lines: one for older children, farther away from the hoop, and one for younger children, closer to the hoop.

How to Play

1. Have participating children get in a line.
2. The children should take turns shooting baskets. The first time a child makes a basket, he or she scores the letter "J." As that child continues to sink baskets, he or she scores consecutive letters that spell "J-E-S-U-S."
3. If a child misses a basket, he or she does not score.
4. The first child to spell "J-E-S-U-S" wins the game.
5. If time allows, have participants continue to score until each spells "J-E-S-U-S." All children receive a prize.
6. Say, **(Winner's name) won our game today. But God says that we are all winners when we believe in Jesus. "Jesus" is the name above all names.**

Note: Make the game more challenging for older children by having them shoot different kinds of baskets: a lay-up shot, a one-handed shot or shots from different angles.

Marshmallow Munch Ages 3-12

Bible Reference: God is our help, Psalm 46

Overview

Children of all ages face adversity. In this game, children will try to munch a marshmallow that is constantly moving. They will be reminded that God can help them with troubles even when their circumstances are difficult.

Helpers: 2

- one person to set up marshmallows on the clothesline
- one person to shake clothesline, cheer for children and award prizes

Materials

- ❏ marshmallow chicks or bunnies
- ❏ dental floss
- ❏ clothesline
- ❏ resealable plastic bags
- ❏ prizes

Preparation

1. Stretch a clothesline across your play area about 6-7' above the floor.
2. Cut 1-2' lengths of dental floss. Tie one end of a floss length securely around each chick or bunny's head. Prepare at least one marshmallow treat per child.
3. To keep the marshmallows fresh, store them in resealable plastic bags until you tie them to clothesline.
4. Tie the marshmallows to clothesline, spacing them about 18" apart. Make sure they dangle at varying lengths to accommodate different children's heights.

How to Play

1. Have the children line up in front of the clothesline, each matched with a treat hanging at his or her mouth level.
2. Explain to the children that the object of the game is to eat the marshmallow treat. Tell them that the clothesline will be jiggling, so the marshmallows will not be stationary. The children may move around to maneuver the treat into their mouths, but they must keep their hands behind their backs.
3. Have the children begin on your signal. One helper should gently shake the clothesline, making it more difficult for the children to eat the marshmallows.
4. Play should continue until all children have eaten their treats. Ask, **What was the most difficult part of this game?** (possible answers: "not using my hands," "the marshmallow moved all the time," "the clothesline was shaking") **When we have difficult times in our lives, God is always there to help us. He can be our hands when things around us keep changing.**
5. Award each child a prize.

Pin the Palm Branch Ages 3-12

Bible Reference: Jesus' entry into Jerusalem, Matthew 21:1-9

Overview

In a variation of the traditional "Pin the Tail on the Donkey," blindfolded children will attach palm branches to the donkey's path.

Helpers: 2

- one person to blindfold children and hand out palm branches
- one person to help the children attach palm branches and award prizes

Materials

- ❏ large piece of white poster board, 20" x 28"
- ❏ donkey pattern, page 141
- ❏ black or brown permanent marker
- ❏ clear, adhesive-backed plastic
- ❏ palm branch pattern, page 140
- ❏ green construction paper
- ❏ clear tape
- ❏ masking tape
- ❏ blindfold
- ❏ pencils
- ❏ prizes

Preparation

1. Enlarge the donkey pattern onto poster board. (See page 19 for how to enlarge patterns.)
2. Reinforce the donkey image with a brown or black marker.
3. Cover the donkey poster with clear adhesive-backed plastic for durability.
4. Duplicate the palm branch pattern on green paper. Cut out one palm branch per child.

5. Tape the donkey poster to the wall of the play area.
6. Use masking tape to mark two starting lines: one for older children farther away from the wall, and one for younger children closer to the wall.

How to Play

1. Have each child write his or her name on a palm branch.
2. Say, **On the day we now call Palm Sunday, Jesus rode into Jerusalem on a donkey. The crowds cheered for Him and laid palm branches in the road. Today, we are going to try to lay down our palm branches along the donkey's path.**
3. Blindfold the first child. Help the child turn around three times, then give him or her a gentle push toward the donkey poster. Note: Younger children may be afraid to be blindfolded. If so, ask them to walk with their eyes closed.
4. Encourage the children to cheer for each other.
5. The helper at the donkey poster can tape the child's palm branch in place and award the child a prize.
6. Continue until each child has had a chance to play.
7. Say, **See how many palm branches cover the road for Jesus!**

Resurrection Eggs Ages 3-12

Bible Reference: The Easter story, Mark 14–16; John 18-21

Overview

Children will find symbols inside plastic eggs that tell the Easter story.

Helpers: 1

- one person to help the children with eggs and explain each symbol

Materials

- ❏ *Resurrection Eggs* (see *Sources*, page 168)
- ❏ prizes

Preparation

1. Review the Easter story.
2. Make sure the eggs are in the order specified by manufacturer.

How to Play

1. Have the child open the first egg. Ask, **What did you find in this egg? Do you know what this symbol means in the Easter story?** Allow the child to respond. Use the *Resurrection Eggs* booklet to explain the symbol more thoroughly.
2. Repeat this procedure for the remaining eggs.
3. Say, **The last egg is empty. That means we are all winners because Jesus is alive!** Give each child a prize.

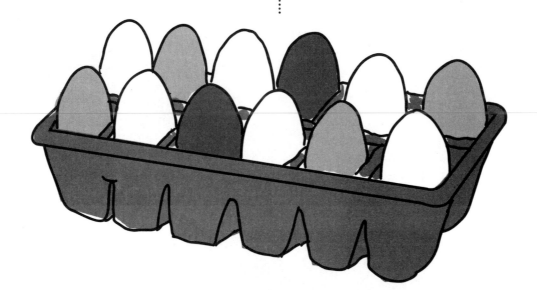

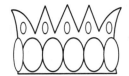

Soul Fishing Ages 3-12

Bible Reference: The Great Commission, Matthew 28:19-20

Overview

Children "go fishing" in a wading pool as an example of Jesus' command to be fishers of men.

Helpers: 2

- one person to distribute fishing poles and prizes
- one person to restock fish and keep the area dry

Materials

- ❏ wading pool or large basin
- ❏ water
- ❏ towels
- ❏ ½"-wide wooden dowels, 24" to 30" long
- ❏ string or twine
- ❏ hot glue gun
- ❏ hook magnets
- ❏ *Soul Fishing* patterns, page 142
- ❏ poster board
- ❏ craft foam or foam meat trays
- ❏ scissors
- ❏ ⅜" nuts, bolts and washers
- ❏ prizes

Preparation

1. Measure 36-40" of twine for each fishing rod. Tie the twine to one end of a dowel and secure with hot glue. Tie a hook magnet to the other end of the twine.
2. Make a template of the *Soul Fishing* patterns. (See page 19 for how to make pattern templates.)
3. Use the template to trace fish onto foam. Cut out the fish.
4. Poke a hole for the fish's eye. Thread a nut and bolt through the hole, securing on each side with a washer.
5. Make several fish to ensure a good "catch."
6. Fill the pool with water. If possible, position the wading pool or basin outdoors. Have plenty of towels ready for drips and spills.

How to Play

1. Explain to the children that they are "going fishing." They will maneuver the magnet on the end of the fishing pole toward the nut/bolt/washer assembly on each fish to make a "catch."
2. Allow the children to catch as many fish as time allows.
3. Say, **After the Resurrection, Jesus told His friends to help others become disciples. He wanted them to go "soul fishing." And He wants us to fish for people, too. Whom do you know who needs to hear about Jesus?**
4. Each child receives a prize.

Springtime Limbo Ages 3-12

Bible Reference: Lean on the Lord, Proverbs 3:5-6

Overview

The children will bend backward while walking beneath a stick. This game will help them understand that they can keep their balance in life by leaning on God.

Helpers: 2

• one person to adjust the stick and blocks
• one person to encourage the children through the line and distribute prizes

Materials

❏ yardstick
❏ two chairs
❏ cardboard blocks or telephone books
❏ crepe paper streamers
❏ *Tissue Paper Flowers*, page 80
❏ clear tape
❏ cassette player and upbeat Christian music
❏ prizes

Preparation

1. Decorate the yardstick with crepe paper streamers and *Tissue Paper Flowers*.
2. Set up the chairs facing each other, about 30" apart. Stack an equal number of blocks or books on each chair until the top measures 46-48" from the floor.
3. Balance the ends of the "limbo stick" on the stacks.

How to Play

1. Explain to the children that they must pass beneath the limbo stick chest-first with their heads leaning back. They may walk through on their feet or their knees, but they cannot slide through on their bottoms. If they touch their hands to the ground or knock the stick off the stacks, they are out.
2. Play lively music in the background as the children pass beneath the limbo.
3. After each child has passed beneath the limbo once, remove one block from each stack and replace the stick. The children can then pass beneath the stick again.
4. Continue to lower the limbo with each round. As the children fall out of the game, award each a prize.
5. The child who passes beneath the limbo at its lowest point without setting down a hand is the winner.
6. Ask, **What was the hardest part of this game?** (possible answers: leaning back, not being able to use my hands, going lower each time, balancing myself) **You could not lean on anything when you went under the limbo. But the Bible tells us that we can keep our balance in life by leaning on God.**

The Road Through Jerusalem

Ages 3-12

Bible Reference: Jesus' entry into Jerusalem, Matthew 21:7-11

Overview

On Palm Sunday, the crowds in Jerusalem covered the roads with their garments as Jesus rode by on a donkey. In this relay race, children will cover their "roads" with clothing, too.

 ## Helpers: 1

• one person will give instructions, referee and hand out prizes

 ## Materials

❏ old clothing such as shirts, jackets, jeans and sweaters
❏ masking tape
❏ prizes

 ## Preparation

1. With masking tape, create two parallel "roads" on the floor, each about 18" wide.
2. Mark a starting line at one end of the roads and a finish line at the other.
3. Place a pile of clothing at each starting line.

How to Play

1. Divide the children into two teams. Have them line up behind the starting lines.
2. Say, **On Palm Sunday, Jesus rode through Jerusalem on a donkey. While He passed through the city, the crowds laid their garments on the road as a sign of worship. Here you see the road through Jerusalem. Your job is to cover the road with clothing because we want to worship Jesus, too.**
3. On your signal, the first child on each team should select a garment and lay it in the road. Once the first child returns to the starting line, the second child can take his or her turn, and so on. Garments must lie flat on the road with the edge of one piece touching the next, so that the road gets covered completely.
4. The first team to cover the road all the way to the finish line wins. All participants receive a prize.

The Way to the Cross Ages 3–12

Bible Reference: *Jesus carries His cross, John 19:17 and Mark 15:21*

Overview

This variation of miniature golf demonstrates that Jesus (and, later, Simon of Cyrene) carried the cross through the streets of Jerusalem to Golgotha.

Helpers: 1

- one person to give instructions and distribute prizes

Materials

- ❏ boxes in various sizes
- ❏ 2-liter plastic soda bottles
- ❏ brown grocery bags
- ❏ clear or brown mailing tape
- ❏ door patterns, page 144
- ❏ palm tree patterns, page 145
- ❏ cross pattern, page 121
- ❏ poster board
- ❏ green, yellow and white craft foam
- ❏ scissors
- ❏ hot glue gun
- ❏ practice golf balls (hollow plastic)
- ❏ child-size golf clubs
- ❏ masking tape
- ❏ prizes

Preparation

1. Make templates of the door, palm tree and cross patterns. (See page 19 for how to make pattern templates.) Plan on making one palm tree for every two buildings.
2. To transform each box into a building in Jerusalem, cut off the box top flaps so that the box will stand without wobbling. Use the door template to trace and cut out a door on either side of the box.

3. Cover each box with brown grocery bag paper and tape. Reinforce the doors with extra tape because these are the openings through which children will hit the balls.
4. To transform a plastic soda bottle into a palm tree, cut off the bottom so the bottle stands without wobbling. Use the door template to trace and cut out an opening on either side of the bottle.
5. With the palm tree template, cut trunks from yellow craft foam and branches from green craft foam. Use a hot glue gun to attach these to each bottle.
6. Use a remaining box to create the cross "hole." Cover the box with brown paper and tape. Cut only one door opening in this box. Use the cross template to cut a cross from white craft foam. Attach it to the box with the hot glue gun.
7. Set up your boxes and palm trees in a miniature-golf type course. Place the cross as the final hole. Mark a starting point with masking tape.

How to Play

1. Give the child a golf club and ball. Explain that the object of the game is to hit the ball through all the "holes."
2. Say, **These buildings and palm trees represent the streets of Jerusalem. After His trial, Jesus (and, later, Simon of Cyrene) carried the cross through the city to the place where He was crucified.**
3. Give each child a prize once he or she reaches the cross hole.

Who Betrayed Jesus? Ages 3-12

Bible Reference: The twelve disciples, Matthew 10:2-4

Overview

This beanbag game teaches children about the 12 disciples. Participants will toss a money bag into the jug that signifies Judas, Jesus' betrayer.

 Helpers: 1

• one person to hand out moneybags, coach children and distribute prizes

 Materials

❏ 12 plastic gallon-size milk jugs
❏ ruler
❏ scissors
❏ stapler
❏ *Disciples' Name Tags*, page 146
❏ craft foam or poster board
❏ permanent marker
❏ craft glue
❏ dark fabric or felt
❏ pennies
❏ rubber bands
❏ masking tape
❏ prizes

Preparation

1. Wash and dry milk jugs thoroughly. Mark a line around the middle of each jug 4" from its bottom. Cut off the top of each jug along that line.
2. Arrange the milk jug bottoms into three rows of four. Staple the assembly together.
3. Reproduce the *Disciples' Name Tags* onto craft foam or poster board. Cut apart the name tags and glue them to the inner sides of the milk jugs that will face the players.

4. Cut three 8" x 8" fabric squares. Place 15 pennies in the center of each square. To complete the money bags, gather their edges and secure each square with a rubber band.
5. Set the milk jug assembly on a low table or flat surface in your play area.
6. Use masking tape to mark two tossing lines: one closer to the milk jug assembly for younger children and one farther away for older children.

How to Play

1. Have each child stand behind the appropriate line. Say, **Jesus had 12 special friends called "disciples." But one of those friends betrayed Him in exchange for a bag of money.**
2. Give the child the three money bags. Say, **Toss the money bag into the betrayer's jug.** If a younger child knows that Judas betrayed Jesus but cannot read the names, help him or her by identifying the correct jug.
3. If the child tosses a money bag into a jug other than the one labeled "Judas," share the appropriate information from page 146.
4. When a child tosses a money bag into the correct jug, say, **Yes, that is right: Judas is the disciple who betrayed Jesus.**
5. Award each child a prize.

Crafts

Beautiful Badges Ages 3-12

Bible Reference: Proclaim the Good News, Mark 16:15

Overview

The children will make buttons that proclaim the Good News of Easter.

Helpers: 1

• one for every 3-4 children

Materials

❏ badge kit (see *Sources*, page 168)
❏ markers or crayons
❏ badge patterns, page 147

Preparation

1. Duplicate the badge patterns for the children to color.
2. Using the manufacturer's instructions, practice making several sample badges so you will be able to assemble badges quickly for waiting children.

What to Do

1. Have the children select and color a badge pattern. They may also wish to create their own original Easter designs.
2. Assemble the children's badges.
3. After you assemble a child's button, attach it to his or her clothing. Say, **Before Jesus went to heaven, He told His disciples to proclaim the Good News to the rest of the world. Wearing this button is one way you can tell others the Good News that Jesus is alive!**

Bunny Bags Ages 3-12

Bible Reference: Storing God's Word in our hearts, Proverbs 2:1-5

Overview

The children will make a carry-home bag that reminds them to store up God's Word in their hearts.

Helpers: 1

• one for every 3-4 children

Materials

❑ white paper lunch bags, 6" x 11"
❑ *Bunny Bag* pattern, page 148
❑ poster board
❑ pink construction paper
❑ pink felt
❑ 15mm (or larger) wiggle eyes
❑ white chenille wire
❑ 1" pink pompons
❑ cotton balls
❑ self-stick paper reinforcements
❑ crayons or markers
❑ craft glue
❑ scissors
❑ ruler or tape measure
❑ Easter basket grass

Preparation

1. Make a template of the *Bunny Bag* pattern on poster board. (See page 19 for how to make pattern templates.)
2. Trace and cut the *Bunny Bag* pattern on white lunch bags. Open up the bags and trim off the extra set of ears along the sides of the bags.
3. Trace and cut out the inner ears from pink construction paper.
4. Trace and cut out the mouths from pink felt.
5. Measure and cut chenille wire into 6" lengths.

6. For each child, you will need: one bag, two inner ears, two wiggle eyes, three 6" chenille wires, two reinforcements, one pink pompon, one pink felt mouth and one cotton ball.

What to Do

1. Help the children poke two holes in the center of the bag's front side, using either chenille wire tips or scissors tips. Show how to affix reinforcements to the holes to prevent ripping.
2. Demonstrate how to weave a chenille wire through one hole from the front to the back, then through the other hole to the front to create the bunny's whiskers. Once the children weave through three wires, show them how to spread out the whiskers slightly by bending them outward.
3. Have the children glue the inner ears, eyes, pompon nose and felt mouth to the bunny's face. They can color on these face parts with markers or crayons.
4. Tell the children to turn over the bunny and glue the cotton ball tail onto the back of the bag.
5. Give the children some Easter basket grass to fill the bag.
6. Ask, **Did you know that this bag is like your heart?** Allow the children to respond. Say, **You can use your *Bunny Bag* to store the crafts, prizes and eggs you receive so that you don't lose anything today. In the same way, God wants us to store up His Word — the Bible — in our hearts so that we can know how to live the right way.**

Bunny Ears Ages 3-12

Bible Reference: *The crippled beggar who jumped for joy, Acts 3:1-10*

Overview

The children will make a set of *Bunny Ears* and use them to jump for joy in praise to God.

Helpers: 1
• one for every 5-6 children

Materials

❑ white poster board
❑ pink construction paper
❑ *Bunny Ears* pattern, page 149
❑ cotton balls
❑ markers or crayons
❑ ruler
❑ scissors
❑ craft glue
❑ stapler
❑ clear tape

Preparation

1. Make pattern templates of the *Bunny Ears* pattern using poster board. (See page 19 for how to make pattern templates.)
2. Trace and cut the outer ears from white poster board. Trace and cut the inner ears from pink construction paper. You will need a set of both inner and outer ears for each child.

3. Prepare the headbands by cutting one 2½" x 24" strip of white poster board for each child.

What to Do

1. Show the children where to glue the inner ears to the outer ears. Have them decide where they want their ears positioned on the headband.
2. Older children may staple the ears themselves. Help the younger ones staple on the ears. Cover the staples with clear tape to avoid injury.
3. Allow the children to glue cotton balls on the outer ears around the pink inner ears.
4. Fit the headband around each child's head and staple the ends together to secure. Cover the staples with clear tape to avoid injury.
5. Say, **The crippled beggar jumped for joy when he was healed. At Easter, we jump for joy to praise God. Can you show me how you can jump for joy with your *Bunny Ears*?**

Butterfly Bookmark Ages 3-12

Bible Reference: *The Living Word, 1 Peter 1:23-25*

Overview

The children will make a bookmark from felt that they can use in their Bibles.

Helpers: 1

- one for every 4 children

Materials

- ❏ felt in assorted colors
- ❏ scissors
- ❏ craft glue
- ❏ *Butterfly Bookmark* pattern, page 150
- ❏ poster board
- ❏ pencils or markers

Preparation

1. Make templates of the *Butterfly Bookmark* pattern using poster board. (See page 19 for how to make pattern templates.)
2. Trace and cut the bookmark and butterfly body parts pieces from felt. You will need one complete set for each child.

What to Do

1. Have the children glue the butterfly to one end of a bookmark.
2. Help the children attach the body parts to the butterfly.
3. Have the children create decorations for the butterfly's wings from scraps of felt. They can use the patterns on page 150 or design their own patterns. They should glue the decorations on the butterfly's wings.
4. Show how to fringe the bottom of the bookmark.
5. Say, **Butterflies are a symbol of new life. Through God's Word — the Bible — we can learn how to have new life in Jesus. Do you have a Bible at home that you can read? Use your butterfly bookmark in your Bible to remind you that God brings you new life through His Word.**

Carrot Pin Ages 3-12

Bible Reference: The Passover meal, Luke 22:8-13

Overview

The children will make a carrot pin and learn about The Last Supper.

Helpers: 1

• one for every 4-5 children

Materials

❑ 12" orange chenille bumps
❑ green chenille wire
❑ scissors
❑ pin backs
❑ pencils or thin dowels
❑ craft glue or glue gun

Preparation

1. Cut the orange chenille bump in half, leaving each half with two bumps. You will need one 6" length for each child.
2. Cut green chenille wire into 3" lengths. You will need four 3" lengths for each child.

What to Do

1. Have the children bend the orange chenille bump in half, creating the carrot.
2. Give each child four 3" lengths of green chenille wire. Show how to lay the wires in a stack, then twist the stack in the center to fasten them together.
3. Demonstrate how to lay the green chenille wire stack on top of the carrot. Twist the top of the orange part of the carrot over the greenery to secure it.
4. Let the children "frill" the green carrot top by wrapping the ends of the wire around a pencil or dowel, creating curlicues.
5. Help the children glue a pin back to the back of the carrot. A glue gun will allow the pin to dry more quickly, but should only be used by an adult.
6. Ask, **Why are carrots popular at Easter?** (possible answers: bunnies eat them; they grow in our gardens; they are food for rabbits) Say, **Yes, bunnies get a nice meal from carrots. Jesus ate a special meal right before Easter. He and His friends shared a dinner called the Passover in a place called the Upper Room.**

Chick Pencil Topper Ages 3-12

Bible Reference: We are God's children, 1 John 3:1

Overview

The children will make a chick and learn that they are God's children.

Helpers: 1

- one for every 3-4 children

Materials

- ❑ yellow and orange felt
- ❑ 1½" yellow pompons
- ❑ yellow feathers
- ❑ 6-7 mm wiggle eyes
- ❑ yellow-painted pencils
- ❑ *Chick Pencil Topper* patterns, page 151
- ❑ poster board
- ❑ scissors
- ❑ craft glue
- ❑ hot glue gun

Preparation

1. Make templates of the *Chick Pencil Topper* patterns using poster board. (See page 19 for how to make pattern templates.)
2. Cut two chick bodies from yellow felt for each child. Cut one beak from orange felt for each child.

What to Do

1. Give each child two yellow feathers. Demonstrate how to trim the feathers to about 1½", and then glue them onto one of the yellow felt chick bodies to make the chick's wings.
2. The children should then glue a yellow pompon on top of the yellow feathers in the center. Help them make the chick's face by attaching wiggle eyes and a beak to the pompon.
3. Have the children lay the eraser end of the pencil in the center of the second yellow felt chick body. An adult should drop hot glue onto the body.
4. Allow the children to attach the first yellow felt chick body to the second.
5. Say, **Who are a chick's parents?** (the hen and the rooster) **We have parents too — our moms and dads. The Bible tells us that we are also children of God.**

Coffee Filter Butterfly Magnet

Ages 3-12

Bible Reference: A new creation in Christ, 2 Corinthians 5:17

Overview

The children will make a butterfly magnet and learn that they can be a new creation in Christ.

Helpers: 1

- one for every 3-4 children

Materials

- ❑ paper coffee filters
- ❑ spring-type clothespins
- ❑ green chenille wire
- ❑ 5-7 mm wiggle eyes
- ❑ self-stick magnetic strips
- ❑ bright-colored poster paint
- ❑ paintbrushes
- ❑ food coloring
- ❑ eyedroppers, one for each color
- ❑ craft glue
- ❑ small bowls
- ❑ water
- ❑ measuring spoons
- ❑ old newspapers
- ❑ string

Preparation

1. Cut the chenille wire into 5-6" strips, two per child.
2. Cut the self-adhesive magnets into 2" strips, one per child.
3. Paint the clothespins and allow them to dry thoroughly. You will need one clothespin for each child.
4. Spread a thick layer of newspapers over your work area.
5. Use string to fashion a small clothesline.

6. To create watercolors, combine 1 tablespoon of water and 8 drops of food coloring in a small bowl. Fewer drops make a lighter color; more drops make a more intense color.

What to Do

1. Give each child a paper coffee filter. Show the children how to fill the eyedropper with a watercolor and release the drops onto the filter. They should wait for the liquid to spread after each drop. Instruct the children that they may cover the whole filter with watercolor, but not soak it.
2. Help the children hang the coffee filters to dry on the clothesline. Allow about 20 minutes' drying time.
3. While the filter dries, show how to twist the chenille wire around the tip of the clothespin (butterfly body) to form antennae.
4. Have the children glue a magnet strip onto back of the butterfly body, and eyes onto the butterfly face.
5. Show how to gather the dried filter in the center, then insert and glue it into the clothespin. Help the children adjust the gathers to look like butterfly wings.
6. Ask, **How does a butterfly start out?** (as a caterpillar) **But the caterpillar changes into a new creation: a beautiful butterfly. That's what happens to us when we trust in Jesus. We become new creations, too.**

Cotton Ball Sheep Ages 3-12

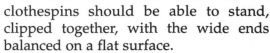

Bible Reference: The Good Shepherd, John 10:1-11

Overview

The children will make a sheep and learn that Jesus is the Good Shepherd.

Helpers: 1

• one for every 3-4 children

Materials

❑ spring-type clothespins
❑ cotton balls
❑ black poster paint
❑ paint brushes
❑ white felt
❑ *Cotton Ball Sheep* ear pattern, page 151
❑ poster board
❑ white chenille wire
❑ ruler
❑ 5-7 mm wiggle eyes
❑ 5 mm (¼") black pompons
❑ hot glue gun
❑ craft glue
❑ pencils

Preparation

1. Paint the lower ½" of the clothespin tips black. These will be the sheep's feet.
2. Clip two clothespins together at the center, crossing like a tepee (see illustration at right). The

clothespins should be able to stand, clipped together, with the wide ends balanced on a flat surface.

3. With a hot glue gun, attach the two sets of clips together at their centers. You will need one clothespin assembly per child.
4. Make a template of the *Cotton Ball Sheep* ear pattern using poster board. (See page 19 for how to make pattern templates.)
5. Cut the sheep's ears from white felt, one set per child.
6. Cut the chenille wire into 3" lengths. Twist the wire around a pencil, creating a curlicue. You will need one per child.

What to Do

1. Let the children glue cotton balls onto the clothespin assembly to create the sheep's body.
2. Show where to attach the sheep's felt ears, wiggle eyes, pompon nose and chenille wire tail with glue.
3. As the children work, say, **Sheep are very special to Jesus. In the Bible, He calls Himself "The Good Shepherd." He says that we are His sheep and that He will give His life for us.**

Cottontail Basket Ages 3-12

Bible Reference: God gathers His believers, Matthew 12:30

Overview

The children will make a small basket and learn about evangelizing.

Helpers: 1

• one for every 3-4 children

Materials

❑ poster board or construction paper
❑ *Cottontail Basket* patterns, pages 152-153
❑ cotton balls
❑ hole punch
❑ scissors
❑ craft glue
❑ clear tape
❑ Easter basket grass

Preparation

1. On poster board or construction paper, duplicate the *Cottontail Basket* pattern and parts for each child.
2. Cut out the *Cottontail Basket* and parts for younger children. Score them on the dashed lines.
3. With a hole punch, cut out two bunny eyes for each child.

What to Do

1. Have the older children cut out a *Cottontail Basket* and parts along the solid lines, then score and fold along the dashed lines.
2. Show the children how to fold the basket together.
3. Help them tape the tabs to the insides of the basket, and tape the handle to the basket's top perimeter.
4. Have the children fringe the bunny's whiskers.
5. They should glue on the bunny's face, face parts, then the cotton ball tail on the back.
6. Give the children some plastic grass to fill their baskets. Say, **We use Easter baskets to gather eggs. In the Bible, God tells us that He wants us to help Him gather people so that they can learn about Jesus. You've learned that Jesus is alive. Whom can you tell?**

Duct Tape Donkey Ages 3-12

Bible Reference: Jesus' entry into Jerusalem, Matthew 21:1-11

Overview

The children will make a donkey puppet to remind them of Jesus' entry to Jerusalem.

Helpers: 1

• one for every 3-4 children

Materials

❑ paper towel tubes
❑ toilet tissue tubes
❑ duct tape
❑ *Duct Tape Donkey* patterns, page 154
❑ poster board
❑ 15 mm wiggle eyes
❑ black or brown construction paper
❑ white paper
❑ clear tape
❑ stapler
❑ craft glue
❑ scissors

Preparation

1. On one end of a paper towel tube, cut two 1½" slits. The slits should be opposite each other, creating two flaps. Fold one flap into the tube.
2. Fit a toilet tissue tube over the folded flap. With duct tape, secure the toilet tissue tube to the paper towel tube at a 90-degree angle.
3. Make templates of the *Duct Tape Donkey* patterns using poster board. (See page 19 for how to make pattern templates.)
4. Trace and cut a mane, ears and tail from black or brown construction paper. Cut the teeth from white paper.
5. You will need one tube assembly and one set of donkey parts for each child.

What to Do

1. Help the children staple a folded mane along the dashed line, then fringe it with scissors by cutting the fold.
2. Show how to fold the mane flaps outward along the dotted line. They can use clear tape to affix the mane to the donkey's back.
3. Have the children fold the ears in half. Point out where they should attach ears to the donkey using clear tape.
4. Help the children cover their donkeys with strips of duct tape.
5. Show where to fold the teeth along the dashed line. They should tape the donkey's teeth to the inside of the toilet paper tube (the donkey's mouth).
6. Demonstrate how to fringe the donkey's tail. They should tape the tail to the inside of the paper towel tube.
7. Allow the children to glue eyes onto the donkey's face.
8. Say, **The donkey is a special part of the Easter story. On the first Palm Sunday, Jesus rode through Jerusalem on a donkey while the crowds waved and cheered for Him.**

Egg Carton Cross  Ages 3-12

Bible Reference: Jesus is alive, Acts 1:3

Overview

The children will make crosses that are a symbol of Jesus' death and resurrection.

Helpers: 1

• one for every 3-4 children

Materials

❑ cardboard egg cartons, dozen-size
❑ poster or acrylic paints
❑ paint brushes
❑ paper cups
❑ craft glue
❑ *Egg Carton Cross Banner*, page 155
❑ ¾" ribbon or construction paper
❑ scissors
❑ markers
❑ old newspapers
❑ smocks (men's old shirts work well)

Preparation

1. Cut the lids and flaps off of the egg cartons and discard the lids and flaps.
2. Cut each carton into two lengthwise strips, each having six egg compartments. Trim off one egg compartment from one of the strips.
3. To assemble the cross, place the shorter strip perpendicular across the longer strip, fitting the center egg compartment of the shorter strip over the third egg compartment of the longer strip. Glue into place. Prepare one cross assembly for each child.
4. Using the *Egg Carton Cross Banner* pattern and markers, make banners for each child from ribbon or construction paper.
5. Spread newspaper over your work area.
6. Fill paper cups with water to rinse paint brushes.

What to Do

1. Have the children wear smocks for this activity.
2. Let the children paint their *Egg Carton Crosses*. Remind them to rinse their paintbrushes in the paper cups when they change colors.
3. As the children paint, ask, **Why do you think the cross is a symbol of Easter?** Give the children time to answer. **Yes, Jesus died on the cross. But the story doesn't end there. On Easter morning, we learn that Jesus is alive.**
4. Allow the crosses to dry.
5. Instruct the children to glue the banners onto the cross arms.

Eggshell Mosaics Ages 3-12

Bible Reference: Jesus took our sins, Isaiah 53:5

Overview

The children will use crushed eggshells that represent Jesus' death for us on the cross.

Helpers: 1

• one for every 4-5 children

Materials

❏ eggshells
❏ bowls
❏ food coloring
❏ vinegar
❏ measuring cup
❏ slotted spoon
❏ paper towels
❏ rolling pin or food processor
❏ plastic containers
❏ *Eggshell Mosaic Cross* and *Egg* patterns, pages 134 and 135
❏ construction paper or poster board
❏ glue
❏ newspaper

Preparation

1. Wash the eggshells thoroughly.
2. To dye eggshells, mix ½ cup boiling water, ½ cup vinegar and 8-10 drops of food coloring in a bowl. Let the eggshells soak in this mixture for 3-5 minutes.
3. Remove the eggshells with a slotted spoon onto paper towels. Keep the colors separate.
4. When the eggshells are completely dry, finely crush them using a rolling pin or food processor with a steel blade.

5. Store the eggshells in plastic containers, one for each color.
6. Duplicate the *Eggshell Mosaic* patterns on construction paper or poster board. You will need one pattern per child.
7. Cover your work area with newspapers.

What to Do

1. Allow each child to select an egg or cross pattern.
2. Show the children how to spread a thin coat of glue on one section of the mosaic pattern.
3. Demonstrate how to sprinkle eggshells over the glued section, covering it completely.
4. Help the children shake off the excess shells.
5. Have the children repeat this process until their mosaics are finished. Say, When Jesus was put on the cross, the guards whipped Him and stuck a spear and nails in Him. Jesus bled, then died. The Bible describes this by saying He was "crushed" for us.
6. Ask, **What did we do to the eggshells in order to use them in the mosaics?** (possible answers: we colored them; we crushed them; we smashed them) **Yes, these eggshells had to be crushed for us to use in these beautiful pictures. And Jesus was crushed for us, too.**

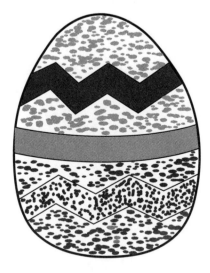

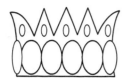

Emmaus Sunglasses Ages 3-12

Bible Reference: Jesus appears on the Emmaus road, Luke 24:13-32

Overview

The children will make sunglasses to learn how Jesus helps us see things differently.

Helpers: 1

• one for every 3-4 children

Materials

- ❏ *Emmaus Sunglasses* patterns, page 156
- ❏ poster board
- ❏ colored poster board
- ❏ colored cellophane or Mylar
- ❏ markers
- ❏ ⅜" wide elastic
- ❏ ruler
- ❏ scissors
- ❏ craft glue
- ❏ stapler
- ❏ clear tape

Preparation

1. Make a template of the *Emmaus Sunglasses* patterns on poster board. (See page 19 for how to make pattern templates.)
2. Trace and cut out the sunglasses from colored poster board, making sure to cut out the lens holes along the dashed lines. You will need one per child.
3. Trace and cut out lenses from colored cellophane or Mylar, two per child.
4. Measure and cut 14" lengths of elastic, one per child.

What to Do

1. Allow the children to decorate the sunglasses with markers.
2. Have them glue the lenses to the backsides of the lens holes.
3. Help the children staple elastic ends to the sunglasses shafts. Adjust the fit as needed. Give the children pieces of clear tape to cover the staple tips.
4. Say, **After the Resurrection, Jesus appeared to two disciples on the road to Emmaus. However, they did not recognize Him immediately. After Jesus spent some time with them, they realized who He was. Jesus helped them see things differently.**
5. Help the children put on their sunglasses. Ask, **How do things look with your sunglasses on?** Allow the children to respond. **These sunglasses remind us that when we walk with Jesus, as did the Emmaus disciples, Jesus can help us see things differently, too.**

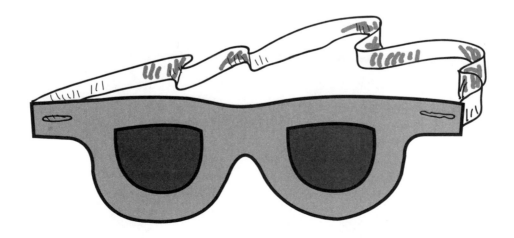

Gumstick Butterfly Ages 3-12

Bible Reference: New life in Christ, Romans 6:4

Overview

The children will make a butterfly from a gum stick and learn that God can make anyone beautiful.

Helpers: 1

• one for every 4-5 children

Materials

❏ packs of gum
❏ pull-apart licorice candy
❏ construction paper
❏ *Gumstick Butterfly Wings* pattern, page 157
❏ poster board
❏ ¾" round adhesive labels, assorted colors
❏ markers or crayons
❏ 7" paper plates
❏ ruler or tape measure
❏ scissors

Preparation

1. Remove the gum sticks from their packages and take off the outer paper wrappers, leaving the gum in the foil wrappers. You will need one gumstick per child.
2. Cut the licorice into 2" lengths, two per child. Separate large ropes into smaller strings.
3. Make a template of the *Butterfly Wings* pattern with poster board. (See page 19 for how to make pattern templates.) Trace and cut out butterfly wings from construction paper, two per child.

What to Do

1. Give each child a paper plate on which to assemble a butterfly.
2. Show the children how to roll tips of licorice strings to create spirals for the butterfly's antennae. Have them press the spiral tips so the antennae won't unravel.
3. Help the children fasten the antennae onto one end of the gum stick (butterfly's body) with a round adhesive label.
4. Let the children decorate the butterfly wings with markers, crayons or round labels.
5. Indicate where to place the wings. Have the children attach the wings to the body with round labels. The children can also decorate the rest of the butterfly's body with round adhesive labels.
6. Say, **This simple piece of gum is now a beautiful butterfly. The Bible tells us that God can take anything and make it into something beautiful — just like you did with this butterfly.**

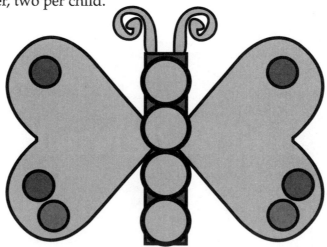

Lamb Mask Ages 3-12

Bible Reference: *Jesus is the Lamb of God, John 1:29*

Overview

The children will make a mask and find out that Jesus is called "The Lamb of God."

Helpers: 1

• one for every 3-4 children

Materials

❏ *Lamb Mask* patterns, page 158
❏ poster board
❏ white poster board
❏ white, pink and black felt
❏ pink yarn
❏ cotton balls
❏ ⅜" wide elastic
❏ stapler
❏ ruler or tape measure
❏ scissors
❏ craft glue
❏ clear tape
❏ old newspapers

Preparation

1. Make a template of the *Lamb Mask* pattern using poster board. (See page 19 for how to make pattern templates.)
2. Trace and cut out the *Lamb Masks* from white poster board, making sure to cut out the eyes along the dashed lines. You will need one mask per child.
3. Cut out the outer ears from white felt, the inner ears from pink felt and the nose from black felt. You will need one set of face parts per child.
4. Measure and cut 3½" lengths of pink yarn, two per child.
5. Measure and cut 14" lengths of elastic, one per child.
6. Spread newspaper over the work area.

What to Do

1. Help the children staple the elastic ends onto the back of the mask behind each ear position. Adjust the fit as needed. Give the children pieces of clear tape to cover the staple tips.
2. Have the children glue the inner ears to the outer ears and affix them to the lamb's face. Point out where to attach a felt nose and yarn mouth.
3. Instruct the children to spread glue across the lamb's forehead. Show how to cover the forehead with cotton balls.
4. Ask, **What is a lamb?** (possible answers: a baby sheep; a fuzzy animal; it says "baaa") **In Bible times, people sacrificed a lamb to God to pay for their mistakes. Jesus never made a mistake, yet He was willing to pay for ours. When He died on the cross, He became the ultimate sacrifice. Because of that, we don't need to give lambs to God anymore. That is why we call Jesus "the lamb of God."**
5. Help the children put on their masks. Guard that they do not go far from your facility wearing the masks because their peripheral vision will be diminished.

Love Bank Ages 3-12

Bible Reference: For God so loved the world, John 3:16

Overview

The children will make a bank that is a reminder of Jesus' love.

Helpers: 1

• one for every 3-4 children

Materials

❏ round, plastic containers, such as frosting cans
❏ wallpaper scraps or samples
❏ fabric scraps
❏ fabric paint
❏ heart and cross patterns, page 157
❏ poster board
❏ flat pan
❏ water
❏ craft glue
❏ scissors
❏ pinking shears
❏ measuring tape

Preparation

1. Remove the labels from the plastic containers. Thoroughly wash and dry the containers. You will need one container for each child.
2. With sharp, pointed scissors, cut a coin slit in the lid of each container.
3. Measure the depth and circumference of each container, adding ½" to the length of the circumference for overlap. Cut a piece of wallpaper for each container to fit this measurement.
4. Make templates of the heart and cross patterns using poster board. (See page 19 for how to make pattern templates.)
5. Use the cross template to cut one cross for each child from fabric scraps.
6. Use pinking shears and the heart template to cut five hearts for each child.

What to Do

1. Fill the flat pan with water. Show the children how to immerse wallpaper into the water, making sure that the paper's adhesive side gets completely wet.
2. Have the children fold the wallpaper rectangle back over itself, right sides out, so the glued sides stick together. Tell them to let the wallpaper sit like this for 2-3 minutes to allow it to "book," or set.
3. Show how to peel apart the wallpaper and apply it to the sides of the plastic container, overlapping the ends at the back. Instruct the children to smooth out the bumps and air pockets with their fingers. The wallpaper will glide easily over the plastic. (For a less messy alternative, allow the children to attach dry wallpaper using craft glue.)
4. Have the children glue one heart onto the wallpapered container and then layer the cross on top of it.
5. Older children can use fabric paint to write "Jesus" above the heart and cross, and their names below it. Assist younger children with the fabric paint.
6. Allow the children to glue the remaining hearts on the *Love Bank* wherever they wish.
7. Say, **God loves you so much, (child's name), that He gave Jesus to you.**
8. If the children have *Clean Pennies* (page 39), invite them to put the coins in their Love Banks as a reminder of Jesus' love.

Marble Eggs Ages 3-12

Bible Reference: The empty tomb, Mark 16:1-7

Overview

The children will sponge paint plastic eggs.

Helpers: 1

• one for every 4-5 children

Materials

- ❏ plastic eggs
- ❏ sponges
- ❏ enamel paints
- ❏ paper plates (any size)
- ❏ old newspapers
- ❏ scissors
- ❏ oil-based thinner, such as mineral spirits or turpentine
- ❏ paper towels
- ❏ smocks (men's long-sleeved shirts work well)

Preparation

1. Cut the sponges into 1½" squares. Dampen them slightly.
2. Spread newspaper over your work area.
3. Pour 1-2 teaspoons of enamel paint onto paper plates. Keep the colors separate.

What to Do

1. Have the children wear smocks for this activity.
2. Give each child a paper plate on which to work.
3. Have each child select a plastic egg. Help them open the eggs. Say, **What is inside your egg?** (possible answers: nothing; it is empty) **This egg is just like Jesus' tomb — both are empty. Jesus' tomb is empty because He is alive!**
4. Show the children how to dip the sponges into paint and blot the excess either on the plate or on paper towels.
5. Demonstrate how to press the sponge onto a closed egg and release it, creating a textured (or "marbled") finish. Explain that they should not drag the sponge as they do when painting with a brush because that will make a smooth finish instead. The children may want to use more than one color on an egg.
6. When the children are finished painting, allow their eggs to dry on their paper plates. They may wish to make a *Bunny Bag* (page 58) or *Cottontail Basket* (page 65) to hold their eggs.
7. As the children clean their hands with the oil-based thinner and paper towels, ask, **What does the outside of your egg resemble?** (possible answers: marble; rock; it's pretty) **Jesus' tomb also had a rock in front of it. But God rolled that stone away when Jesus arose from the dead!**
8. Have the children wash their hands to remove the mineral spirits.

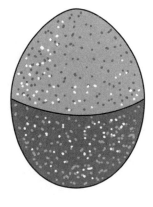

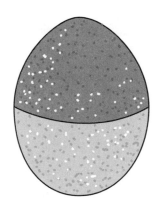

Palm Branch Ages 5-12

Bible Reference: Jesus' entry into Jerusalem, John 12:12-15

Overview

The children will make a palm branch that can be used in church on Palm Sunday or taken home.

 ## Helpers: 1

• one for every 3-4 children

 ## Materials

❑ green construction paper, 9" x 12"
❑ toilet tissue tubes
❑ clear tape
❑ green markers
❑ scissors
❑ measuring tape

 ## Preparation

1. Measure the height and circumference of the toilet tissue cardboard tubes. Add ½" to the circumference measurement.
2. Cut rectangles of green construction paper measuring the height by the adjusted circumference.
3. You will need one cardboard tube, one pre-cut rectangle and four additional 9" x 12" sheets of green construction paper for each child.

 ## What to Do

1. Have the children prepare the palm branch stem by taping the green rectangle around the toilet tissue roll. Or have the children color the tissue roll with green markers.
2. Give each child four sheets of green construction paper. They should lay the sheets on the table lengthwise, overlapping each sheet about one inch over the next.

3. Have the children tape the sheets where they overlap, creating one long, continuous sheet of green.
4. Help the children roll their long sheets into a tube, starting at one end and continuing the length of the connected paper. When finished, tape one end of the tube. Leave the other end free.
5. Have the children cut four to six slits lengthwise down the construction paper tube, beginning at the untaped end. They should cut through all layers of paper. The slits should extend halfway down the tube.
6. Help the children pull out the center of the untaped end (the "palm branch") to create the palm leaves.
7. They should then crush the taped end of the palm branch, stuff it into the prepared toilet tissue cardboard tube (the "branch stem") and tape to secure it.
8. Say, **On the first Palm Sunday, Jesus rode a donkey into Jerusalem. The crowds waved palm branches and shouted "Hosanna!" as He rode by. Show me how you can wave your palm branch and shout for Jesus.**

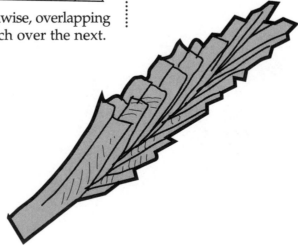

Peter's Rooster Ages 3-12

Bible Reference: Peter denies Christ, Luke 22:54-62

Overview

The children will make a rooster with feathers and tissue paper.

Helpers: 1

• one for every 3-4 children

Materials

- ❑ *Peter's Rooster* pattern, page 159
- ❑ poster board
- ❑ colored feathers
- ❑ yellow and red tissue paper
- ❑ 12-13 mm moveable plastic eyes
- ❑ brown chenille bumps
- ❑ jumbo craft sticks
- ❑ scissors
- ❑ craft glue

Preparation

1. Duplicate *Peter's Rooster* on poster board for each child.
2. Cut out the roosters. Glue one jumbo craft stick to the back of each rooster. Allow the glue to dry completely.
3. Cut yellow and red tissue paper into 2" squares.
4. Cut the brown chenille bumps into two bump lengths.

What to Do

1. Distribute the roosters to children. Help them glue feathers to the rooster's tail section.
2. Show the children how to fold the two-bump brown chenille in half to create the rooster's legs. Point out where the children should attach the legs to the rooster's body.
3. Demonstrate for the children how to crunch each 2" square of tissue paper into a cluster.
4. The children should glue red clusters to the rooster's beak and comb, then cover the rooster's head and body with yellow clusters.
5. Have the children glue a plastic eye onto the rooster's head.
6. As the children work, ask, **Do you know the significance of the rooster in the Easter story?** Allow time to respond. **Peter was one of Jesus' disciples. After Jesus was arrested, Peter pretended that he didn't know Jesus. He pretended more than once — he did it three times! After the third time, the rooster crowed, just as Jesus said it would. Peter realized that he had made a big mistake, but even so, he knew that Jesus still loved him.**

Plastic Wrap Flower Stick

Ages 3-12

Bible Reference: The Word of God stands forever, Isaiah 40:8

Overview

The children will make flowers and learn that God says real flowers die, but His Word is forever.

Helpers: 1

• one for every 3-4 children

Materials

❏ clear and colored plastic wrap
❏ ruler or measuring tape
❏ red jelly beans
❏ rubber bands
❏ 10" bamboo skewers
❏ hot glue gun or craft glue

Preparation

1. Cut one 6" square of clear plastic wrap per child.
2. Tear off six 12" squares of colored plastic wrap and two 12" squares of green plastic wrap per child.
3. Tear off three 3" strips of green plastic wrap per child.
4. Count out eight jelly beans for each child.
5. Plug in the hot glue gun.

What to Do

1. Give each child six 12" squares of colored plastic wrap to make flower petals. Show how to make a petal by laying a square on a flat surface and folding it into thirds so that the plastic sticks to itself, then smooth out the resulting 4" wide strip.
2. Show how to double over the strip so that its cut edges meet. They can twist the cut ends of each petal into a "tail." Repeat this method to make six petals.
3. Give each child a 6" square of clear plastic to make a flower center. Have the children place the jelly beans in the middle of the square. Help them bring all four corners of the plastic together and twist the ends together into a tail.
4. Allow the children to arrange the petals and center to look like a flower. Demonstrate how to twist all of the tails together. They can use a rubber band to secure the flower on its underside.

5. Show how to poke a bamboo skewer into the bottom of the flower to make a stem. Glue the skewer in place with craft glue, or use a glue gun to hasten drying.
6. Give each child two 12" squares of green plastic wrap and have them make leaves as they made petals. They can twist the cut ends of each leaf into a tail to attach to the flower's "stem" (skewer).
7. Have the children fold the 3" green plastic wrap strips lengthwise to 1½" wide and smooth them out. Help them wrap the flower's stem with these green strips, beginning at the base of the flower.
8. The children can attach the leaves to the stem by holding the leaf tails against the skewer while overlapping both the tail and skewer with plastic.
9. Show how to secure the end of the green plastic wrap to the tip of the skewer with craft glue, or an adult can use a glue gun to hasten drying.
10. Say, **It's fun to pick flowers in the spring. But once we pick flowers, what happens to them? The flowers you made today will last a long time. They remind me of the Bible. God says flowers will die someday, but His Word will last forever.**

Resurrection Rainbow Ages 3-12

Bible Reference: *A rainbow is a sign of hope, Genesis 9:12-16*

Overview

The children will make a rainbow as a sign of hope.

Helpers: 1

• one for every 3-4 children

Materials

❏ plastic wrap in five colors: pink, yellow, green, blue, purple
❏ poster board or construction paper
❏ *Resurrection Rainbow* pattern, page 160
❏ craft glue
❏ scissors

Preparation

1. Duplicate the *Resurrection Rainbow* for each child on poster board or construction paper.
2. Tear 5" wide strips of each color of plastic wrap. Cut each strip into four pieces.
3. Cut out the *Resurrection Rainbows* for younger children.

What to Do

1. Have the older children cut out a *Resurrection Rainbow*.
2. Demonstrate how to gather each small piece of plastic wrap into a cluster.
3. Have the children glue plastic clusters onto the rainbow's arches, beginning in the center of the rainbow and working outward in prism order: pink, yellow, green, blue and purple.
4. Have the children glue yellow clusters onto the cross.
5. Say, **God gave us the first rainbow as a sign of hope. At Easter, we are reminded about the best hope of all — Jesus is alive!**

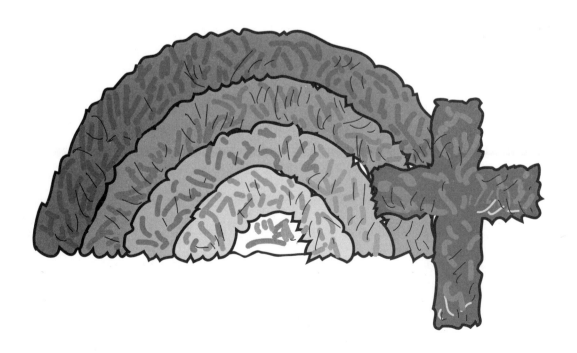

Salvation Bracelet Ages 3-12

Bible Reference: Salvation through faith, Ephesians 2:8

Overview

The children will make a bracelet that tells the story of salvation.

 ## Helpers: 1

• one for every 3-4 children

 ## Materials

❏ 2 mm hemp, suede or craft cord
❏ 8-9 mm pony beads in black, red, white, blue, green, yellow and clear
❏ resealable plastic sandwich bags
❏ *Salvation Story*, page 161
❏ scissors

 ## Preparation

1. Cut the hemp, suede or craft cord into 16" lengths. You will need one length for each child.
2. Duplicate the *Salvation Story* and place one copy in a resealable plastic sandwich bag for each child.

 ## What to Do

1. Give each child a plastic bag containing the *Salvation Story*. Tell the children to follow along with the story as they make their bracelets. As you help the children make knots or hand them each colored bead, explain the symbolic meanings as listed below.
2. Show how to tie a knot about 7" from one end of the cord. Then hand each child one colored bead at a time to slide onto the cord.
3. After the children thread on all six of the colored beads, have them tie a knot at the end so the beads will be secured in the center of the bracelet.
4. Have the children string a clear bead onto the bracelet, then string the opposite end of the cord through the clear bead from the other side. Help the children tie knots at both ends of the cord. The bracelet is now adjustable and can fit any size wrist.
5. Invite the children to wear their bracelets. Say, **Now you can tell the Salvation Story to your family and friends by using your bracelet!**
6. Have the children take their *Salvation Story* bags with them so they can refer to them, look up the Bible verses at home and store their bracelets in them.

First knot: reminds us of when were born.

Black: We all are sinners and make mistakes.

Red: Jesus paid for those mistakes by dying on the cross.

White: We are forgiven and cleansed because of Jesus.

Blue: the water that is used when we are baptized.

Green: Keep growing closer to God by praying, reading the Bible and attending church.

Yellow: the glory of heaven, when we will be with Jesus.

Second knot: One day our lives will end and we will meet God.

Clear: Jesus' clear call to put our faith in Him.

Spring Flower Basket Ages 3-12

Bible Reference: God created everything, Revelation 4:11

Overview

The children will assemble and decorate a basket to remind them of God's creation at springtime.

Helpers: 1

• one for every 3-4 children

Materials

- ❑ colored 8⅞" foam plates
- ❑ curling ribbon or yarn
- ❑ construction paper
- ❑ *Spring Flower Basket* patterns, page 162
- ❑ poster board
- ❑ hole punch
- ❑ scissors
- ❑ craft glue

Preparation

1. Make templates of the *Spring Flower Basket* pattern using poster board. (See page 19 for how to make pattern templates.)
2. Make the bottom layer of the basket by tracing the handle template onto a plate and cutting it out.
3. Make the top layer of the basket by cutting a second plate in half.
4. Turn the plate half bottom side up on the first plate, creating the basket pocket.
5. With a hole punch, make holes every 1½" around the perimeter of the plates, punching two holes simultaneously when you get to the basket pocket section.
6. For each basket, cut a 60" length of curling ribbon or yarn.
7. You will need one basket assembly for each child.
8. Trace and cut the *Spring Flower Decorations* from construction paper.

What to Do

1. Give each child two basket pieces and ribbon or yarn. Demonstrate how to "sew" together the two plates to assemble the basket. The children can use either a running stitch or a whip stitch.
2. Help the children tie a bow at the top of the basket when it is put together.
3. Let the children decorate their baskets with *Spring Flowers* and glue.
4. They can also fill their baskets with *Tissue Paper Flowers* (page 80) or *Plastic Wrap Flower Sticks* (page 76).
5. Say, **God created everything. During the spring, we see the beauty of His creation when plants and flowers come to life. What do you like most about spring?**

Tissue Paper Flowers Ages 3-12

Bible Reference: Consider the lilies, Luke 12:27-28

Overview

The children will make flowers to remind them of God's care.

Helpers: 1

• one for every 5-6 children

Materials

- ❏ colored tissue paper
- ❏ green chenille wire
- ❏ ½" or ¾" pompons
- ❏ *Tissue Paper Flowers* pattern, page 163
- ❏ poster board
- ❏ scissors
- ❏ craft glue
- ❏ ruler

Preparation

1. Make a template of the *Tissue Paper Flower* pattern using poster board. (See page 19 for how to make pattern templates.)
2. With the template, cut squares from tissue paper. You will need four squares for each flower.
3. Cut the chenille wire into 6" lengths. You will need one length for each flower.

What to Do

1. Have the children select four squares of tissue paper. Show how to stack the squares so that all edges are even.
2. Tell the children to treat the stack as one piece of tissue paper. Demonstrate how to fold the stack accordion-style, with each crease about ½" deep.
3. Help the children twist the end of a 6" chenille wire around the middle of the folded stack.
4. With scissors, show how to trim the ends of the folded stacks into a point or petal shape.
5. Show how to fan out the stack and separate each piece of tissue to make the flower's petals. Caution the children to handle the tissue carefully to prevent ripping.
6. Allow the children to glue a pompon in the center of the flower.
7. Say, **Aren't these flowers beautiful? The Bible reminds us that God cares about us even more than flowers, and He will always provide for us.**

Note: This craft works well when paired with *Spring Flower Baskets*, page 79. Or use *Tissue Paper Flowers* on *Spring Vines*, page 28, to decorate your facility.

Wallpaper Butterfly Ages 3-12

Bible Reference: *Hope through Jesus, 1 Peter 1:3*

Overview

The children will make a butterfly out of wallpaper and discover that God can use us in ways we cannot imagine.

Helpers: 1

• one for every 3-4 children

Materials

❑ wallpaper scraps
❑ *Wallpaper Butterfly* patterns, pages 163-164
❑ poster board
❑ scissors
❑ chenille wire
❑ ruler or measuring tape

Preparation

1. Make templates of the *Wallpaper Butterfly* pattern using poster board. (See page 19 for how to make pattern templates.)
2. Trace and cut the upper and lower wings from wallpaper. You will need one set for each child.
3. Cut the chenille wire into 6" lengths, one per child.

What to Do

1. Show the children how to make the butterfly's upper wings. Begin in one corner and fold the square accordion-style, making the creases about ¼" deep.
2. Have the children fold the lower wings in a similar way, this time beginning on one curved side and folding accordion-style across the width of the wings.
3. Help the children gather both sets of wings in their centers. Show how to twist the chenille wire around both wing centers to secure them together.
4. Allow the children to bend the ends of the chenille wire into the shape of antennae.
5. Demonstrate how to spread the butterflies' wings out from the folds.
6. Say, **What is wallpaper used for?** (possible answers: to decorate walls; to make a room look better) **But this wallpaper is not on a wall. Instead, it was used for something else — it became a butterfly. This butterfly is just like the hope God gives us in Jesus. If we let Him, God can use us in ways we cannot imagine.**

Snacks

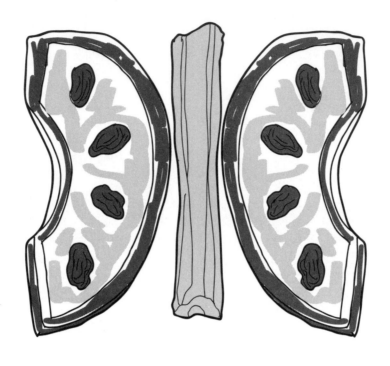

Apple Butterflies Ages 3-12

Bible Reference: New life in Christ, Romans 6:4

Overview

Make a snack that represents new life in Jesus.

Helpers: 1

• one for every 3-4 children

Materials

❑ apples
❑ celery
❑ peanut butter
❑ raisins
❑ paring knife
❑ plastic knives
❑ paper plates

Preparation

1. Halve and core the apples.
2. Cut the apples into slices, which will become the butterflies' wings. You will need two apple slices per child.
3. Cut the celery into sticks to use as the butterflies' bodies.

What to Do

1. If the children are helping, instruct them to wash their hands before preparing the food.
2. Give each child a paper plate, two apple slices and a celery stick. Show them how to arrange the pieces into the shape of a butterfly.
3. Have the children use plastic knives to spread peanut butter onto each apple slice.
4. They can decorate butterflies' wings with raisins.
5. As the children eat their snack, say, **Butterflies begin a new life when they emerge from their cocoons. When we trust Jesus, we begin a new life, too.**

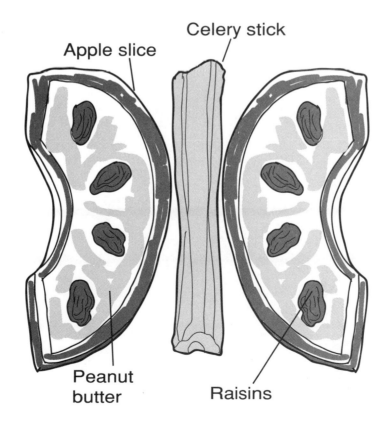

Apple slice
Celery stick
Peanut butter
Raisins

Chick Cracker Ages 3-12

Bible Reference: We are God's children, John 1:12

Overview

The children will decorate a snack cracker and learn that they are God's children.

 Helpers: 1
• one for every 3-4 children

 Materials
❑ round snack crackers
❑ cheddar cheese spread
❑ chopped black olives
❑ carrots
❑ paper plates
❑ plastic knives
❑ carrot peeler
❑ paring knife

 Preparation
Peel the carrots and chop them into small triangles.

What to Do

1. If the children are helping, instruct them to wash their hands before preparing food.
2. Give each child a paper plate, a cracker and a plastic knife. Show them how to spread some cheese smoothly across the cracker.
3. Point out where the children should place the two chopped olives (for the chick's eyes) and carrot triangle (for the chick's beak).
4. As the children eat their crackers, ask, **How are we like chicks?** Allow them to respond. **Chicks are children chickens. They have parents — the hen and the rooster. When we believe in Jesus, we become children of God.**

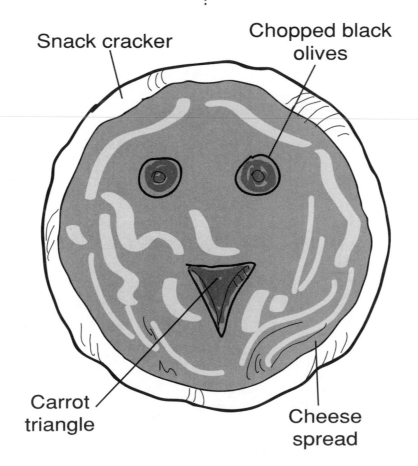

Snack cracker

Chopped black olives

Carrot triangle

Cheese spread

Cross Toast Ages 3-12

Bible Reference: The cross, John 19:17-18

Overview

The children will make cinnamon toast in the shape of a cross.

Helpers: 1

• one for every 5-6 children

Materials

- ❑ sliced bread
- ❑ granulated sugar
- ❑ cinnamon
- ❑ liquid butter or margarine
- ❑ cross cookie cutter
- ❑ toaster or toaster oven
- ❑ measuring cup and spoon
- ❑ plastic knives
- ❑ plastic spoons
- ❑ salt or sugar shaker
- ❑ paper plates

Preparation

In a small bowl, mix together ¼ cup of granulated sugar and 1 teaspoon of cinnamon. If desired, pour the mixture into a salt or sugar shaker.

What to Do

1. If the children are helping, instruct them to wash their hands before preparing food.
2. Toast the bread in a toaster or toaster oven.
3. Place each slice of toast on a paper plate. Allow the children to cut cross shapes from toast with a cookie cutter.
4. Give the children plastic knives. Help them drizzle and spread butter or margarine onto their cross toast.
5. The children can sprinkle cinnamon sugar onto their toast with a shaker or a spoon.
6. While they are eating, ask, **Why is the cross such an important symbol at Easter?**

Fruit Trios Ages 3-12

Bible Reference: The crucifixion, Matthew 27:38

Overview

The children will make a fruit snack that symbolizes Jesus on the cross between the two robbers.

Helpers: 1

• one for every 5-6 children

Materials

❑ pineapple chunks, fresh or canned
❑ maraschino cherries
❑ toothpicks
❑ paper plates

What to Do

1. If the children are helping, instruct them to wash their hands before preparing food.
2. Drain the fruit.
3. On each toothpick, thread a pineapple chunk, a maraschino cherry and another pineapple chunk. Make sure the cherry is in the middle.
4. As the children eat say, **Jesus was crucified between two robbers. Just as we pierced the fruit with a toothpick, He was pierced for us.**

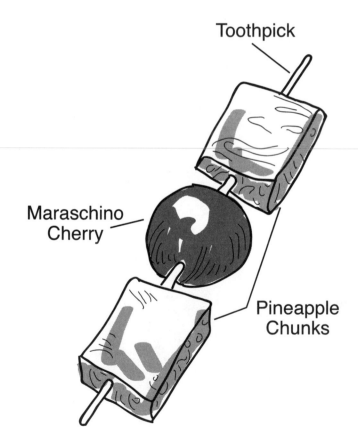

Toothpick

Maraschino Cherry

Pineapple Chunks

Jelly Bean Prayer Ages 3-12

Bible Reference: God is love, 1 John 4:8-10

Overview

The children will assemble jelly beans to tell about Jesus.

Helpers: 1

• one for every 5-6 children

Materials

❏ jelly beans
❏ snack-size resealable plastic bags
❏ *Jelly Bean Prayer*, below
❏ scissors

Preparation

Duplicate the *Jelly Bean Prayer* for each child.

What to Do

1. If the children are helping, instruct them to wash their hands before preparing food.
2. Have each child cut out the *Jelly Bean Prayer* and place it in a resealable plastic bag so that they can see it as they work.
3. Show them how to select jelly beans of each color as they read the prayer (you will need to read it aloud for younger children). Have them put the jelly beans in the bag and seal it. Provide extra jelly beans for snacking.
4. As the children eat their snack, say, **This prayer reminds us that Jesus is the King, the Creator, the Light and the Way. Most of all, He is Love. Which is your favorite kind of jelly bean?**

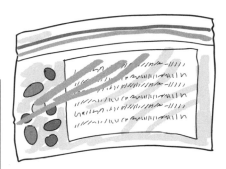

Jelly Bean Prayer

Purple reminds me that You are the King.

Green reminds me that You made everything.

Orange reminds me You create each new day.

Yellow reminds me You are the Light and the Way.

Black reminds me of the sins I have done.

White reminds me that through You, they're all gone.

Red reminds me on the cross, You shed blood.

Pink reminds me that You are Love.

Thank You for **jelly beans**, they're more than a treat —

They're a promise of hope, a promise so sweet!

Lamb Cookies Ages 3-12

Bible Reference: Jesus is the lamb of God, John 1:29

Overview

The children will decorate a cookie to look like a lamb, a symbol of Jesus.

Helpers: 1

• one for every 5-6 children

Materials

❑ round cookies, such as sugar cookies or oatmeal cookies
❑ cheesecake-flavored cream cheese or prepared white frosting
❑ shredded coconut
❑ large marshmallows
❑ miniature marshmallows
❑ chocolate chips
❑ red candy dots
❑ kitchen scissors
❑ plastic knives
❑ paper plates

Preparation

With kitchen scissors, cut large marshmallows lengthwise into fourths.

What to Do

1. If the children are helping, instruct them to wash their hands before preparing food.
2. Give each child a cookie on a paper plate and a plastic knife.
3. Show how to spread cream cheese or frosting onto one side of cookie.
4. Let the children sprinkle coconut over the frosting to create the lamb's "wool."
5. Show where to position two marshmallow fourths on each side of the frosted cookie for the lamb's ears. Instruct the children to put three miniature marshmallows along the top of the cookie for the lamb's forehead.
6. Have the children use two chocolate chips for the lamb's eyes and a red candy for the lamb's nose.
7. As the children eat, say, **Lambs are born in springtime. That is one reason why they are so popular at Easter. But there is another reason. Jesus is our Savior, and He is also called the Lamb of God.**

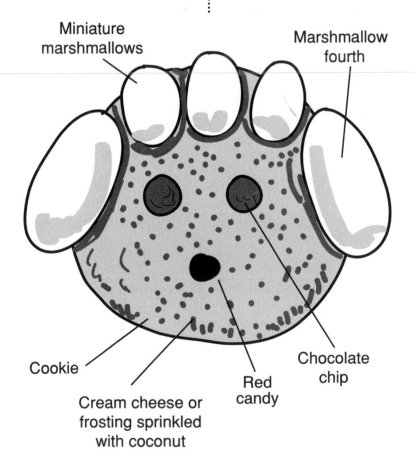

Miniature marshmallows

Marshmallow fourth

Cookie

Cream cheese or frosting sprinkled with coconut

Red candy

Chocolate chip

Orange Sunshines Ages 3-12

Bible Reference: Jesus is the Light of the world, John 8:12

Overview

The children will make a sunshine face from fruit and learn that Jesus is the Light of the world.

 Helpers: 1
• one for every 5-6 children

 Materials
- ❑ seedless oranges
- ❑ seedless grapes or drained maraschino cherries
- ❑ cutting board
- ❑ knife
- ❑ paper plates

 Preparation

1. Slice an orange in circles, leaving the rind intact. The circles will become sun faces.
2. Cut an orange in half, then in wedges, leaving the rinds intact. The wedges will become the sun rays.
3. Cut grapes or cherries into halves and quarters.

What to Do

1. If the children are helping, instruct them to wash their hands before preparing food.
2. Give each child a paper plate, an orange circle and some orange wedges. Show how to arrange the wedges around the circle to resemble a sun's rays.
3. Let the children place grape or cherry halves on the sun's face for eyes. Demonstrate how to put grape or cherry quarters in a line to make a smile.
4. As the children eat, ask, **What does the sun do for us?** (possible answers: it gives us light; it brings warmth). **Jesus said that He is the Light of the World. How is Jesus like the sun?**

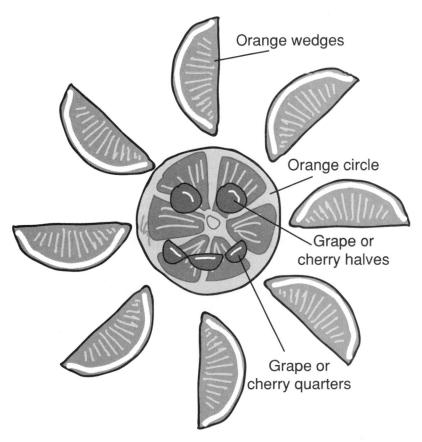

Orange wedges

Orange circle

Grape or
cherry halves

Grape or
cherry quarters

Rainbow Pretzels Ages 3-12

Bible Reference: *A rainbow is God's promise, Genesis 9:12-16*

Overview

The children will make a pretzel snack and learn about God's promise.

Helpers: 1

• one for every 5-6 children

Materials

- ❏ thin pretzels
- ❏ chocolate chips
- ❏ margarine
- ❏ rainbow decors or nonpareils
- ❏ double boiler
- ❏ forks
- ❏ plate
- ❏ waxed paper

What to Do

1. If the children are helping, instruct them to wash their hands before preparing food.
2. In a double boiler, melt together one cup of chocolate chips and one tablespoon of margarine, stirring continually until smooth.
3. While the chocolate melts, pour decors or nonpareils onto a plate. Spread waxed paper on a counter nearby.
4. Work on the pretzels one at a time. With a fork, submerge a pretzel into the melted chocolate. Lift it out and allow the excess chocolate to drip off.
5. Lay the pretzel on the decors or nonpareils, allowing the candies to stick to the chocolate.
6. Transfer the pretzel to waxed paper.
7. When all the pretzels have been dipped and decorated, allow them to harden in the refrigerator. One cup of chocolate chips coats about 16-18 pretzels.
8. As the children eat the pretzels, say, **These pretzels are covered with colors of the rainbow. A rainbow is God's promise to us that He will love us forever. What rainbow colors can you see on your pretzel?**

Candy décors or nonpareils

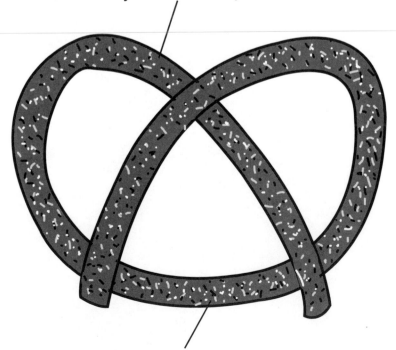

Chocolate-covered pretzel

Upper Room Snack Mix Ages 3-12

Bible Reference: The Upper Room, John 13 and Mark 14:1-26

Overview

The children will make a snack mix that teaches about the disciples' time with Jesus in the Upper Room.

Helpers: 1

• one for every 5-6 children

Materials

- ❑ peanuts
- ❑ raisins
- ❑ semi-sweet chocolate chips
- ❑ miniature marshmallows
- ❑ measuring cup
- ❑ mixing bowl
- ❑ wooden spoon

What to Do

1. If the children are helping, instruct them to wash their hands before preparing food.

2. Say, **On the night before He died, Jesus spent some special time with His disciples in the Upper Room. They shared a meal together.**

3. Help the children measure out one cup of chocolate chips and pour them into the bowl. Say, **These chips are semi-sweet. The time in the Upper Room was bittersweet for Jesus. He loved being with His disciples, but He knew He would be leaving them soon.**

4. Help the children measure out one cup of miniature marshmallows and pour them into the bowl. Say, **While in the Upper Room, Jesus washed the disciples' feet. This took a great deal of humility. He wanted to show the disciples how to be true servants of God and have pure hearts. The white marshmallows represent Jesus' purity.**

5. Help the children measure out one cup of peanuts and pour them into the bowl. Say, **After Jesus washed the disciples' feet, Judas left the Upper Room. Jesus knew that Judas was leaving in order to betray Him. Judas had a hard heart, just like these peanuts have a hard texture.**

6. Help the children measure out one cup of raisins and pour them into the bowl. Say, **After Judas left, Jesus served the disciples bread and wine. Wine is made from grapes. Did you know that raisins are also made from grapes? These raisins represent that bread and wine, or "communion" as we call it, that Jesus shared with His disciples.**

7. Have the children take turns mixing the snacks in the bowl. As they eat the snack, say, **When Jesus and the disciples were finished in the Upper Room, they went to the Garden of Gethsemane.**

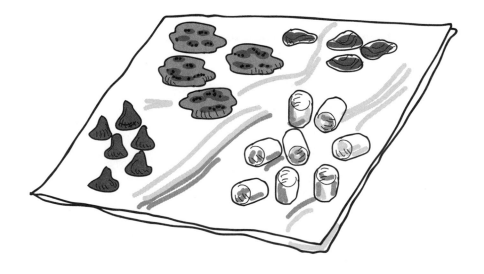

More Activities!

Balloon Hats Ages 3-12

Bible Reference: The gift of the Holy Spirit, John 20:21-22

Overview

Breath and wind are symbols for the Holy Spirit. Jesus "breathed" the Holy Spirit into His followers and they were transformed into dynamic Christians. Similarly, children will see balloons filled with air and transformed into colorful Easter headwear.

Helpers: 2

- one person to inflate balloons
- one person to make a hat and interact with each child

Materials

- ❑ high-quality pencil balloons, 2" x 60"
- ❑ balloon pump
- ❑ permanent marker

Preparation

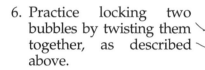

1. Stretch the balloons before you begin to inflate them.

2. Do not fill the balloons completely, but always leave a "tail" to allow air to expand when you twist.

3. Tie off the balloons after inflation.

4. Practice twisting the balloons into bubbles. Use one hand to twist the balloons and the opposite hand to hold the bubbles. Twist all bubbles in the same direction to prevent unraveling.

5. Twist bubbles several times to secure.

6. Practice locking two bubbles by twisting them together, as described above.

7. Select one or two balloon hat designs below. Practice each one several times until you can make a hat while talking with another person.

Bee Bonnet

Bible Reference: The sweetness of God's Word, Psalm 119:103

What to Do

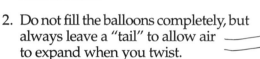

1. Have the child select a balloon. Inflate it, leaving a 3" tail, which will become the bee's stinger.

2. As you work, say to the child, **After the Resurrection, Jesus filled His disciples with the Holy Spirit, just as I am filling this balloon with air.**

3. Twist off a 1" bubble at the tied end of the balloon. Wrap the rest of the balloon around the child's head to test for fit. Twist off a second bubble at the proper length.

4. Lock the second bubble to the first bubble to create a headband.

5. Twist off a 1" bubble at the tail end of the balloon to create a bee's head with stinger. Lock the bee's head onto the headband.

6. Twist the remaining balloon loop into two equal parts to make wings. Lock the wings onto the bee's head joint.

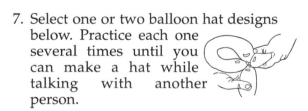

7. With a permanent marker, draw two eyes on the bee's head.

8. Ask, **What does a bee eat?** Allow the child to respond. **Yes, bees like to eat sweet nectar from flowers. And the Bible says that God's Word is sweeter to us than honey.**

9. Fit the Bee Bonnet onto the child's head.

Cross Headband

Bible Reference: Take up your cross, Luke 9:23

What to Do

1. Have the child select two balloons. Inflate both almost completely, leaving only tiny tails.
2. As you work, say, **After the Resurrection, Jesus filled His disciples with the Holy Spirit, just as I am filling this balloon with air.**
3. Holding one balloon lengthwise, find its center. Place this point at the child's forehead and wrap both ends of the balloon around to the back of the child's head. Twist off a bubble on both ends of the balloon at the point where they meet.
4. Lock the two bubbles together to create a headband. Adjust the bubbles horizontally so that they become the cross' arms.
5. Twist a second balloon into two bubbles: one about one-third the length of the balloon, the second about two-thirds the length of the balloon. Lock this second balloon onto the headband joint. Adjust it so that the shorter bubble becomes the upper part of the cross and the longer bubble is the lower part of the cross.
6. Say, **Jesus died so that we might live with Him forever. In order to live with Him, we must "take up the cross." That means we need to believe in Jesus and do what He wants us to do.**
7. Help the child put on the Cross Headband so that the cross portion is at child's back. Say, **(Child's name), take up your cross!**

Easy Bunny Ears

Bible Reference: "He who has ears," Mark 4:23-24

What to Do

1. Have the child select a balloon. Inflate the balloon, leaving a 2" tail.
2. As you work, say to the child, **After the Resurrection, Jesus filled His disciples with the Holy Spirit, just as I am filling this balloon with air.**
3. Holding the balloon lengthwise, find its center. Place this point under the child's chin.
4. Wrap the balloon up around the child's head so that the balloon frames the child's face. This will ensure a proper fit.
5. Twist off bubbles at both ends of the balloon at the point where they meet on the top of the child's head. These bubbles will become the ears.
6. Lock two ears together and adjust them so that they point upward.
7. Say, **Jesus often said, "He who has ears, let him hear." Jesus wanted us to be sure to listen carefully to what He said so that we could live the right way.**
8. Fit the Bunny Ears onto the child's head. Say, **You have ears now. Make sure you listen carefully to Jesus!**

King of Kings Crown

Bible Reference: Jesus is the King of kings, Revelation 19:16

What to Do

1. Have the child select three balloons. Inflate one balloon, leaving a 3-4" tail. Inflate the remaining two balloons almost completely, leaving about 1" tails on each.
2. As you work, say to the child, **After the Resurrection, Jesus filled His disciples with the Holy Spirit, just as I am filling these balloons with air.**
3. Twist off a 1" bubble at the tied end of the first balloon. Wrap the rest of the balloon around the child's head to test for fit.

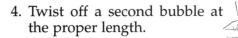

4. Twist off a second bubble at the proper length.

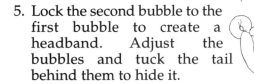

5. Lock the second bubble to the first bubble to create a headband. Adjust the bubbles and tuck the tail behind them to hide it.

6. Twist off a 1" bubble at the tied end of one of the remaining balloons. Lock it onto the headband joint (at the 12:00 position) on the headband circle. Twist off a 1" bubble at the other end of the balloon. Lock this bubble onto the headband at a point directly opposite the first joint (at 6:00), to complete half of the "crown."
7. Twist off a 1" bubble on the last balloon. Lock this bubble onto the headband at 3:00.
8. Twist off a bubble at the middle of this third balloon. Lock it at the midpoint of the other arching balloon to create the center tip of the crown.
9. Twist off a 1" bubble at the remaining end of the balloon. Lock this bubble onto the headband at the spot directly opposite the last joint, or at 9:00, on the headband.
10. Say, **In the Bible, Jesus is called "The King of Kings." This means that He is more powerful than any other king or ruler. Wear this crown in honor of Him!**
11. Fit the crown onto the child's head.

Swan Hat

Bible Reference: The Holy Spirit transforms us, 2 Cor. 3:17-18

What to Do

1. Have the child select a balloon. Inflate the balloon, leaving a 3-4" tail.
2. As you work, say to the child, **After the Resurrection, Jesus filled His disciples with the Holy Spirit, just as I am filling this balloon with air.**
3. Twist off a 1" bubble at the tied end of the balloon. Wrap the rest of the balloon around the child's head to test for fit. Twist off a second bubble at the proper length. Lock the second bubble to the first bubble to create a headband.
4. Create the swan's neck and beak from the remaining length of balloon. Hold the tail in one hand and bend it downward. With the other hand, grasp the balloon about 1" from the tail and squeeze hard, forcing air into the tail and creating a curve for the neck. Adjust as needed.
5. With a permanent marker, draw two eyes on the swan's head.
6. Ask, **Do you know the ugly duckling story?** Allow the child to respond. **When the ugly duckling grew up, he became a beautiful swan. When we believe in Jesus, the Holy Spirit works in our hearts to turn us into something beautiful, too.**
7. Fit the Swan Hat onto the child's head.

Oversize Bunny Ears

Bible Reference: God is attentive to us, Psalm 34:15

What to Do

1. Have the child select three balloons. Inflate one balloon, leaving a 3-4" tail. Inflate the remaining two balloons almost completely, leaving about 1" tails on each.
2. As you work, say to the child, **After the Resurrection, Jesus filled His disciples with the Holy Spirit, just as I am filling these balloons with air.**
3. Twist off a 1" bubble at the tied end of the first balloon. Wrap the rest of the balloon around the child's head to test for fit.
4. Twist off a second bubble at the proper length. Lock the second bubble to the first bubble to create a headband. Wrap the tail around the bubbles and tuck the first bubble inside the second. Adjust the unit so that it resembles a puffy cottontail at the back of the headband.
5. The remaining two balloons will become the bunny ears. Construct them one at a time.
6. Twist off a 1" bubble on each end of the first balloon. Find the center in the remaining length. Twist the balloon at this spot to create the tip of the ear.
7. Lock the two 1" bubbles together. Lock the ear onto the headband about 5" from the back of the headband.
8. Repeat steps 5 and 6 for the second ear.
9. Say, **These Bunny Ears are huge, but God's ears are even bigger. The Bible says that God hears every cry we make.**
10. Fit the Bunny Ears onto the child's head.

Face Painting Ages 3-12

Bible Reference: The Lord's commands, *Deuteronomy 6:6-9*

Overview

The Lord instructed the Israelites to tie His commands on their hands and bind them on their foreheads as a way of teaching their children His Law. Likewise, painting Christian symbols on children's cheeks and hands will remind them of God's goodness and promises.

Helpers: 1

• one person to paint designs and interact with each child

Materials

❑ face paint
❑ thin-tipped paintbrush or makeup brush
❑ bowls of water
❑ face paint designs, page 165
❑ white construction paper
❑ clear, adhesive-backed plastic
❑ old newspapers
❑ paper towels
❑ mirror

Preparation

1. Select a few face paint designs from page 165 or create your own.
2. With face paint and paintbrush or makeup brush, practice these designs on construction paper. You will find that a thin-tipped brush makes a clearer design than a wide-tipped brush.
3. On a fresh piece of construction paper, make a sample chart showing the designs you have practiced. Allow the designs to dry. Cover the sheet with clear, adhesive-backed plastic for protection and durability. The children can study this chart to make their selections.

4. Spread newspaper over your work area.
5. Have clean water in bowls. Each time you change colors, rinse your brush and blot it on paper towels.

What to Do

1. Have the child select a design from your sample chart. Find out if the child wants the design painted on his or her cheek or hand.
2. As you work, say, **God wants us to remember His rules. In the Bible, He tells us to not only talk about His commands, but to also tie them on our hands and bind them to our foreheads. That is exactly what we are doing right now as we paint your face (or hand).**
3. Explain the design the child has chosen:
• The cross reminds us that Jesus loves us so much that He died for us.
• The sun reminds us that Jesus is the Son of God. He is also the Light of the world.
• The star reminds us that Jesus is the bright Morning Star.
• The heart reminds us that God is love.
• The fish reminds us that Jesus told us to be fishers of men.
• The flower reminds us that God created the world.
• The rainbow reminds us that we have hope through Jesus.
• The butterfly reminds us that we have new life through Jesus.
4. Hold the mirror so that child can see the finished design on his or her face.

Petting Zoo Ages 3-12

Bible Reference: "Feed My sheep," John 21:15-17

Overview

The children will see and pet animals that represent God's creation.

Helpers: 1 per animal

- owners should designate what care their animals need

Materials

- ❏ guest animals
- ❏ appropriate cages and boxes
- ❏ chairs for pet owners
- ❏ poster board
- ❏ markers

Preparation

1. Locate congregation members, friends or pet store owners who are willing to bring their animals to your celebration. In particular, seek out owners of rabbits, chicks, ducks and other animals closely associated with the spring season.
2. Find out if the animals have any special requirements. Some may be indoor-only pets. Children may be able to hold some animals and simply look at others. Ask the owners to specify their preferences for caring for and feeding their animals.
3. With poster board and markers, make a sign that lists petting rules.
4. Decide where you will put the petting zoo in your set-up. Tell the pet owners your plan and secure their approval.
5. Make sure owners or a qualified assistant will remain with the animals.
6. Help the owners set up cages, boxes and the petting rules poster on the day of your event.

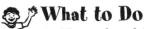
What to Do

1. Have the children enjoy the pets as the pets' owner(s) designates.
2. Say, **(Owner's name) takes good care of his (or her) pets. He (or she) must love them very much. Jesus loves us, too. That is one reason why He told Peter to take care of us, His sheep, after He returned to heaven.**

Piñatas Ages 3-12

Bible Reference: Jesus gave Himself, Galatians 2:20

Overview

The children will participate in a vivid example of Jesus' sacrifice as they strike the piñata and it pours forth prizes and treats.

 ## Helpers: 2

• one person to assist children
• one person to shake the rope

Materials

❑ piñatas
❑ wrapped candies, small toys and prizes
❑ large sticks or baseball bats
❑ ropes
❑ blindfolds

Preparation

1. Provide a piñata for each age group you will host: under 5, ages 5-6, ages 7-9 and ages 10-12, for example. This will allow each child to participate at his or her level of skill. Have one piñata for every 8-10 children so that all youngsters get a turn at batting.
2. Fill the piñatas with wrapped candies, toys and prizes.
3. Designate separate areas of your grounds or facility for each piñata.
4. Attach ropes securely to the piñatas. Tie the ropes to tree branches, portions of a fence, hooks or other reliable anchors.

 ## What to Do

1. Separate the children into appropriate age groups. Lead each group to its designated area.

2. Say, **Each of you will get a turn striking the piñata. What do you think will happen when the piñata breaks?** Allow the children to respond. **Yes, goodies and treats will pour out for all of you. It is just like what Jesus has done for us. Can anyone say why?** Allow the children to respond. **Yes, Jesus emptied Himself completely for us. He pours out His blessings on us when we believe in Him.**

3. Help the children get in a line. Remind them to stand back from the piñata so that no one gets hurt.

4. Hand the first child in line the stick or bat. Blindfold the child and turn him or her around several times.

5. Have the child strike at the piñata. They might need tips such as "Swing higher" or "It is on your left." If the children need more of a challenge, shake the rope to make the piñata move around.

6. Repeat steps 4 and 5 until all children have had a chance to swing.

7. Tell the batting child to stop swinging when the piñata breaks, because the other children will rush forward to gather the treats. Help the batter remove the blindfold quickly so that he or she can participate.

8. Make sure all children find a few candies and prizes.

The Easter Story All Ages

Bible Reference: The Easter Story, Matt. 26-28; Mark 14-16; Luke 22-24; John 18-21

Overview

Present the Easter story to children and their families.

Helpers: 1-?

• varies according to chosen format

Materials

varies according to activity

Preparation

1. Once your team decides how it will present the Easter story (see ideas below), gather appropriate materials.
2. Schedule rehearsals for those involved in the presentation.
3. Reproduce *Egg Hunt tickets* (page 124) to distribute to the children upon conclusion of the story.

Drama with Narration

While this option requires the most preparation, it has great impact because the audience can visualize the Easter story as it unfolds. It is a good choice if you decide to present the story once in a large assembly.

1. Select a rendition of the Easter story from one of the Gospels or combine different accounts into one text. Use an accessible Bible translation, such as the New International Version or the New Revised Standard Version.
2. Type or copy out the text so that it is easy to read. This will be your narrator's script.
3. Have a volunteer with a clear speaking voice serve as narrator for the drama. Remind the narrator to speak slowly and distinctly. If you present the story in a large room or your church sanctuary, make sure the narrator has proper amplification.
4. Recruit helpers to enact the drama, portraying the characters mentioned in the script. Explain to the helpers that they will not need to speak but merely pantomime the narration.
5. Assemble simple Bible-time costumes for actors, such as dishcloths with headbands.
6. Assemble the props needed for your script, such as a cross, a sword, a whip, a rope and a cloth.
7. Rehearse the drama with narration several times so that all participants feel comfortable.
8. Time the drama to make certain that it is 10 minutes or less.
9. Distribute egg hunt tickets to each child at the conclusion of the story.

Flannel Board

Telling the story with flannel board helps children to see it as well as hear it. If your church does not already have a flannel board and flannel figures, see *Sources* on page 168.

1. Choose an individual who is very familiar with the Easter story to make this presentation.
2. Gather the necessary flannel figures.
3. Arrange chairs so that everyone in the audience can see the flannel board.
4. If the presenter has never used the flannel board, show him or her how to gently press figures to the board. The presenter can easily tell the story while putting up and taking down figures.
5. Help the presenter put the figures in the proper order.
6. Have the presenter rehearse the presentation several times with flannel figures.
7. Time the presentation to make certain it is 10 minutes or less.
8. Distribute egg hunt tickets to each child at the conclusion of the story.

Resurrection Eggs

You may elect to use *Resurrection Eggs* as a means of presenting the Easter story rather than as a game station. This method works well with a small group of children, where each can open a few of the eggs.

1. The instructions for *Resurrection Eggs* are on page 50.
2. Distribute egg hunt tickets to each child at the conclusion of the story.

Story Book

Children love story books. This option is suited for both large and small groups.

1. Choose an Easter story book that has clear pictures and a simple text. Consult your pastor, local Christian bookstore or public library for suggestions.

2. Recruit a volunteer with a clear speaking voice to serve as your reader. Remind the reader to speak slowly and distinctly. If you present the story in a large room or your church sanctuary, make sure the reader has proper amplification.
3. Arrange chairs so that everyone in the audience can see the book. If you will be reading the story book to several small groups in succession, consider doing so on a rug with pillows so that children and parents can stretch out and relax.
4. Distribute egg hunt tickets to each child at the conclusion of the story.

Egg Hunt Ages 3-12

Bible Reference: *The parable of the lost sheep, Luke 15:3-7*

Overview

The children will hunt for and collect plastic Easter eggs.

Helpers: varies

- one person to supervise each age group
- several people to hide the eggs

Materials

- ❑ plastic Easter eggs
- ❑ wrapped candies, stickers, small magnets and toys
- ❑ large trash bags
- ❑ extra bags or baskets
- ❑ extra flashlights (if hunting after dark)
- ❑ *Egg Hunt tickets*, page 124

Preparation

1. Decide where you will have your egg hunt. Designate separate areas of your grounds or facility for each age group you plan to host: under 5, ages 5-6, ages 7-9 and ages 10-12, for example.
2. Make certain that your publicity literature states: "Bring your Easter basket." If you are planning an evening event, include "Bring a flashlight." Have extra baskets and flashlights on hand for those who have none.
3. Stuff Easter eggs with candies, stickers, small magnets and toys. Prepare 8-12 eggs per child.
4. Place the eggs for each age group in a separate trash bag so there will be enough to hide in each area.
5. Reserve a bag of extra eggs to give to children who find few or none.

6. Hide eggs shortly before the egg hunt. Do not leave eggs outside overnight since dew might spoil them.
7. Do not use boiled eggs. They can be a health risk.
8. Arrange for the children to receive an Egg Hunt ticket at the Easter story station, the registration table or other venue prior to the hunt.

What to Do

1. Separate the children into age groups. Make sure each child has a bag or basket in which to gather eggs.
2. Collect an egg hunt ticket from each child.
3. Say, **Jesus came to the earth to seek out and save the lost. Today, you are going to seek out Easter eggs!**
4. Remind older children that the younger ones will be escorted to their hunting areas first. Ask them to be considerate of the little ones.
5. Lead groups to their hunting areas, beginning with preschoolers and early elementary ages.
6. Encourage the children as they hunt. Quietly point out a few hiding spots to those who need help.
7. Distribute extra eggs to children who find few or none during the hunt.

Note: Two variations of the traditional egg hunt are described on the next page.

Egg Hunt in the Dark

Bible Reference: *Jesus is the Light of the world, John 8:12*

- -

What to Do

If you have scheduled an evening party, plan to have the children bring flashlights for the egg hunt. This is a big adventure for youngsters!

1. An egg hunt in the dark will take longer than one in daylight, so allow extra time. Review safety rules beforehand and ask the children to take particular caution as they hunt.

2. Before the children begin to hunt, say, **Jesus told us that He is the light of the world. When we follow Him, we will never walk in darkness. Use your flashlight tonight to remind you to always walk with Jesus!**

Mary's Hunt

Bible Reference: *Mary at the empty tomb, Matt. 28:1-10, Luke 24:1-9, John 20:1-18*

- -

What to Do

This hunt illustrates the empty tomb in a striking way. Because younger children might become confused and frustrated by this activity, plan to use it for your 8-12 year-olds only.

1. Prior to the hunt, designate two areas for this group. Hide eggs in only one area. Leave the other empty. Be sure to keep these arrangements a secret.

2. At the beginning of the egg hunt, escort the children to the *empty* section. Let them search for about 5 minutes. When you hear, "I can't find any!" "Where are all the eggs?" and other similar comments, gather the children together.

3. Say, **On Easter morning, Mary went to Jesus' tomb. Can anyone tell me what she found there?** Allow the children to respond. **Yes, the tomb was empty. There are no eggs here as a reminder that Jesus is not in the tomb. He has risen!**

4. Lead the children to the other hunting area and let them find eggs there.

Lessons

Cleaning Up with Jesus All Ages

Bible Reference: Jesus cleanses hearts, Revelation 21:5

Overview

Jesus can make us clean and new on the inside.

Materials

- ❑ materials for *Clean Pennies*, page 39
- ❑ a few shiny, new pennies
- ❑ Bible

Preparation

1. Prepare as for *Clean Pennies*. Make sure you have at least one older, dark penny for each child.
2. For the demonstration, select bright pennies that contrast well with the older ones.
3. Mark Revelation 21:5 in your Bible.

Presentation

1. Hold out the old, dirty pennies in one hand and the new, sparkly pennies in the other. Ask, **What do you see in my hands?** (pennies; some shiny pennies; some dirty ones). **How do you think the dirty pennies got that way?** (they have been used a lot; they are old; they have been near things that have germs). **Why do the shiny pennies look so clean?** (they are new; they have been kept away from things that will dirty them; they haven't been used much yet).

2. Point to the dirty pennies. Ask, **Do you know that we are just like these dirty pennies? Every time we say something nasty to a friend or disobey our parents, we get a little bit dirtier on the inside. When we get angry and hurt someone else's feelings, our insides become a little dirtier, too. That dirt is called "sin."**

3. Say, **But these pennies can be clean once more. Let me show you how.** Give each child a dark penny. Invite them to drop the pennies into the bowls of vinegar mixture one at a time. **Watch and see how the pennies are changing color. They are becoming like new again!**

4. Say, **Do you know that the same thing can happen to you and me? No, we can't climb into this bowl and have our insides made clean. God shines us up in a different way.** Open your Bible to Revelation 21:5. **Jesus said, "I am making everything new."**

5. Say, **This is what Easter is about. When Jesus hung on the cross, He took the punishment for all those things that you have done that are dirtying up your insides. When you tell Jesus you are sorry for those sins, and that you don't want to do them anymore, He will take them away. He will give you a clean, new heart.**

6. Say, **When Jesus takes away everything in your heart that is dirty or messy and leaves your insides fresh and sparkling, you will be even cleaner than these shiny pennies!**

7. Say, **Let's pray together.** Have the children bow their heads. **Jesus, please take away the dirty parts on my insides and make me new again. Thank You for going to the cross so this is possible. Amen.**

8. Give each child an older penny that has been made new. Say, **Keep this penny as a reminder of Jesus' work in you.**

Hosanna All Ages

Bible Reference: Matthew 21:1-9

Overview

Children can cheer for Jesus.

Materials

- ❏ instructions and materials for *Palm Branch*, page 74
- ❏ Bible

Preparation

1. Make a sample Palm Branch.
2. Plan to have the children make their own Palm Branches, or prepare one for each child.
3. Mark Matthew 21:1-9 in your Bible.

Presentation

1. Ask, **Are any of you on a sports team?** (yes, I am in soccer; I like t-ball; no, but I watch my big sister play) **What does the crowd do during a game?** (cheer; shout; clap). **Those are all wonderful ways to encourage your team. Can you name some words that spectators use when they cheer and shout?** (Hooray!; Keep going!; Good job!)

2. Ask, **What kind of words do you use to praise God?** (Thank You, Lord; We worship You; You are mighty and great). **Those are terrific ways to praise God.**

3. Say, **I noticed that you suggested certain phrases to cheer for a team and other phrases to praise God. Why? How is praising God different than cheering for a team?** Allow the children to think about this question. (He is God, not a man; the team is playing a game; God is very powerful) **When we cheer for a team, we encourage them. When we praise God, we worship Him. We thank Him for all He has done and for who He is. Praising Him is a lot like cheering for Him.**

4. Say, **In Bible times, people used special words to cheer for God. I am going to read you a passage from the Bible. See if you can tell me what some of those special praise words are.** Read Matthew 21:8-9. Give the children an opportunity to respond.

5. Say, **Yes, in Bible times, people used the** word "Hosanna." Originally, "Hosanna" meant "Save now!" In other words, when folks shouted "Hosanna!" they were asking for the Lord's help. People learned that they could count on God to answer when they cried for help. So "Hosanna!" became a cheer of praise.

6. Ask, **What do the winning players receive at the end of a tournament or big contest?** (trophies; medals; applause) **In Bible times, there was a special way to honor heroes.** Hold up your sample Palm Branch. **In the Holy Land, there are many palm trees. The palm branch became a symbol of victory.** Wave your palm branch. **When Jesus rode through Jerusalem, people did more than just cheer. They also waved palm branches as a sign of worship to Jesus, their hero and King.**

7. Help the children make palm branches or distribute prepared ones. Say, **Let's cheer for Jesus right now, just like the crowds in Jerusalem did when He rode through the city on a donkey. Remember, there are lots of special words we can use to praise God. Let's use as many as we can think of.** Lead the children in waving palm branches and in shouting, "Hosanna! Hooray for Jesus! Praise God! The Lord is so good!"

8. Say, **Let's pray together.** Have the children bow their heads. **Lord, we praise You because You are God. Thank You, Jesus, for coming to earth and dying on the cross for us. Hosanna to God in the highest! Amen.**

Jelly Beans of Love All Ages

Bible Reference: 1 John 4:8-10

Overview

Jesus has a special kind of love for us.

Materials

- ❏ instructions and materials for *Jelly Bean Prayer*, page 87
- ❏ Bible

Preparation

1. Make a sample *Jelly Bean Prayer* snack to use in the presentation.
2. Plan to have the children assemble their own *Jelly Bean Prayer* snacks, or prepare one for each child to take home.
3. Mark 1 John 4:8-10 in your Bible.

Presentation

1. Ask, **What is your favorite color of jelly bean?** (children will name various colors and flavors) **Why do you like that one?** (it tastes good; it is my favorite color)
2. Bring out the sample *Jelly Bean Prayer* snack. Ask, **What do you see here?** (a bag of candy; all kinds of jelly beans; can we have some?) **Yes, this is an assortment of different colors of jelly beans. But they are not just for snacking. Each jelly bean tells us something special about Jesus.**
3. Select the purple jelly bean and hold it out for the children to see. Say, **In Bible times, only certain people were allowed to wear purple. Does anyone know who had this privilege?** Allow the children time to guess. **Only royalty could wear purple. A man who wore a purple robe was likely a king or prince. So the purple jelly bean tells us that Jesus is a king. But He is not just any king. The Bible says that Jesus is the "King of kings."**
4. Display the green jelly bean. Ask, **Can you name some things that are green?** (grass; trees; flowers; frogs; grasshoppers) **Yes, much in creation is green. The green jelly bean reminds us that God created the world.**

5. Ask, **What colors do you see in a sunrise?** Allow the children to brainstorm, then show the orange and yellow jelly beans. **Orange reminds us that the Lord brings us each new day, just like He gives us the sunrise. And yellow is the color of light. The yellow jelly bean reminds us that Jesus is the Light of the world.**
6. Select the black jelly bean. Say, **Black is the color for sin — the mistakes I make. But because of Jesus,** (exchange the black jelly bean with the white) **my sins are taken away and I am clean again. Jesus died on the cross and shed His blood** (show the red jelly bean) **so that I can be pure and whole.**
7. Say, **Jesus loves us so very much that He was willing to die for us! Listen to what the Bible says.** Read 1 John 4:8-10 from your Bible, then hold out the pink jelly bean. **Pink is the color of love. This last jelly bean stands for the special love Jesus has for us.**
8. Say, **Let's pray together.** Have the children bow their heads. Lead them in the *Jelly Bean Prayer.*
9. Have the children assemble their own *Jelly Bean Prayer* snacks or distribute those you prepared in advance. Say, **Take your prayer home and share it with your families.**

Jesus Breaks Free All Ages

Bible Reference: Matthew 27:57-60; 28:1-6

Overview

Jesus' body was wrapped in cloth and put in a grave but He arose and broke free.

Materials

- ❑ instructions and materials for *Caterpillar Cocoon*, page 38
- ❑ white linen or cotton cloth
- ❑ a paper butterfly, such as *Coffee Filter Butterfly Magnet* (page 63) or *Wallpaper Butterfly* (page 81)
- ❑ Bible

Preparation

1. Have several rolls of toilet tissue so the children can help you "wrap" a cocoon.
2. Mark Matthew 27:57-60 and 28:1-6 in your Bible.

Presentation

1. Hold up the butterfly. Ask, **When a butterfly is first born, does it look beautiful and graceful like this?** (no, it is a caterpillar; no, it is long and skinny with lots of feet). **How does a caterpillar change into a butterfly?** (it wraps itself in a cocoon; it changes while inside the cocoon). **Yes, that's right. A butterfly starts out as a caterpillar. Let's wrap a cocoon right now to see how this happens.** If there are more than four children, divide them into groups.
2. Select one child in each group to be the cocoon. Give a roll of toilet tissue to each remaining child. Show the children how to encircle the cocoon child with tissue to cover him or her completely.
3. Speak to the children who are the cocoons. Say, **When I say, "Butterflies, break free," break out of your cocoons and begin to fly.** Have the children tear off the tissue and become butterflies.

4. Gather the children back together. Say, **Jesus became like a cocoon, too. This is how it happened. When Jesus died on the cross, one of His followers asked for permission bury His body. That man's name was Joseph of Arimathea.** Read Matthew 27:57-60, 28:1-6.
5. Say, **Joseph took Jesus' body and wrapped it in clean, linen cloth — just like a cocoon.** Hold up a sample of cloth. Pass it around so the children can feel it. **Then Joseph put Jesus' body in a tomb that was the size of a small cave. He rolled a large, heavy stone in front of the tomb and went away.**
6. Say, **But Jesus did not stay in His cloth cocoon or in the grave. On Easter morning, Jesus broke free, just like our butterflies did. He showed that He is alive.**
7. Say, **Let's pray together.** Have the children bow their heads. **Jesus, we praise You. You did not stay in the grave, but broke free that we might have new life. Thank You so much. Amen.**

Pretzel Prayer Helper All Ages

Bible Reference: Matthew 6:9-15; Romans 8:34; Romans 8:26-27

Overview

We pray to God the Father, through Jesus and in the Holy Spirit.

Materials

❑ materials and instructions for *Rainbow Pretzels*, page 90
❑ Bible

Preparation

1. Make a sample of *Rainbow Pretzels*.
2. Plan to have children assemble their own *Rainbow Pretzels* snacks, or prepare one for each child.
3. Mark Matthew 6:9-15, Romans 8:34 and Romans 8:26-27 in your Bible

Presentation

1. Display the *Rainbow Pretzel* sample so that all children can see it. Ask, **What do you see here?** (a pretty treat; a chocolate pretzel; may I have some?) **In a little while, we will all get to sample the *Rainbow Pretzels*. But did you know that this pretzel is more than just a delicious snack? This pretzel can teach us a few things about talking with God.**

2. Ask, **How many holes are in the pretzel?** (three) **These holes tell us three different ways God helps us when we pray. When we pray, sometimes we don't know whom we are talking to!** Point to one hole. **Here is our first clue. Jesus said that when we pray, we should talk to our Father who is in heaven.** Read Matthew 6:9-15.

3. Say, **God the Father is listening to us when we pray. Jesus says we should talk to Him all the time. But how can we be sure that He hears us?** Allow the children to respond with their ideas. **Thank you for all of those answers. The Bible gives us the best reason of all.** Read Romans 8:34. Point to the second pretzel hole. **The Bible reminds us how important it is to trust in Jesus and not just in ourselves. When we have faith in Jesus, we can be certain that He is sitting right next to God the Father and praying for us at the same time we are praying.**

4. Say, **When we pray, we talk to the Father** (point to the first pretzel hole) **and through Jesus** (point to the second pretzel hole). **But do you ever have times when you want to pray and you just don't know what to say?** Allow children to respond. **Yes, sometimes we have things to discuss with God and we aren't sure how to say what is on our minds.**

5. Read Romans 8:26-27. Point to the third pretzel hole. Say, **Here is another way God helps us when we pray. The Holy Spirit knows what is going on inside our hearts. So even if we mess up our words when we talk with the Father, He still understands us, thanks to the Holy Spirit.**

6. Say, **So this is what we can learn from our *Pretzel Prayer Helper*: when we pray, we talk to the Father** (point to first pretzel hole), **through Jesus** (point to second pretzel hole) **and in the Holy Spirit** (point to third pretzel hole). **Let's do that right now!** Have the children bow their heads.

7. Pray, **Father, thank You for prayer. Jesus, thank You that we can trust You to help us in everything, even in prayer. Holy Spirit, thank You for understanding our hearts. In Jesus' name, Amen.**

8. If time allows, help the children learn the Lord's Prayer.

9. Distribute prepared *Rainbow Pretzels* or have the children help make them.

The Lamb of God All Ages

Bible Reference: John 1:29

Overview

Jesus is the perfect Lamb of God.

Materials

- ❏ instructions and materials for *Lamb Mask*, page 71
- ❏ low table or chair
- ❏ Bible

Preparation

1. Make a *Lamb Mask* to use in the presentation.
2. If you plan to have the children assemble their own *Lamb Masks*, have materials ready.
3. Situate a low table or chair that will serve as an altar in the presentation area.
4. Mark John 1:29 in your Bible.

Presentation

1. Hold up your *Lamb Mask* so all children can see it. Ask, **What do I have?** (a lamb; a mask; a sheep face) **Does anyone know why lambs are so popular in the springtime?** Allow the children to brainstorm. **Yes, lambs are born in the spring. But there is another important reason why lambs are special this time of year, and especially at Easter: Jesus is the Lamb of God.**

2. Ask, **Does that sound confusing to you? Why?** Allow the children to think out loud (lambs are white and fuzzy and Jesus is not; He is a man and a lamb is a baby; lambs don't talk but people talk). **In order to understand why Jesus is the Lamb of God, we need to know a few things.**

3. Say, **First, let's talk about what happens when we make a mistake. Perhaps you hit your brother or you spoke in a nasty way. What do your parents do when this happens at your house?** (I am punished; I get put in "Time Out"; I must say, "I am sorry") **Yes, there is always a punishment when we make a mistake.**

4. Say, **In Bible times, people had a different way of paying for their mistakes. When a person sinned, he had to take an animal to the priest at the temple. Usually, he took a lamb. It could not be just any lamb. No, this lamb had to be very special. It had to be perfect, with no cuts or bruises.**

5. Say, **The priest would offer the lamb up to God on the altar.** Lay the *Lamb Mask* on the chair or table altar. **The lamb would pay for the person's mistake.**

6. Ask, **But what would happen when that person made another mistake? Yes, he would have to go find another perfect lamb, take it to the temple and offer it to God.**

7. Say, **God loved us so much that He sent us the perfect lamb: Jesus. We don't have to bring animals into church to pay for our mistakes anymore. Jesus took care of them on the cross. He paid the punishment, just like the lambs did.** Read John 1:29.

8. Say, **Let's pray together.** Have the children bow their heads. **Dear Lord, thank You for sending Jesus. Thank You, Jesus, for taking the punishment for me on the cross. You are the Lamb of God. Amen.**

9. If time allows, have the children assemble their own *Lamb Masks*.

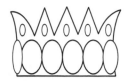

The Second-Chance Friend

All Ages

Bible Reference: John 14-17

Overview

Peter denied Jesus three times, and Jesus forgave him three times.

Materials

- ❑ materials and instructions for *Peter's Rooster*, page 75
- ❑ Bible

Preparation

1. Make a sample *Peter's Rooster*.
2. If you plan to have the children assemble *Peter's Roosters*, have materials ready.
3. Mark John 21:1, 14-17 in your Bible.

Presentation

1. Say, **You probably have lots of friends. Can you name some of them?** Allow the children to respond. **(Child's name), why is (friend's name) your friend?** Ask other children to share why their friends are important to them.

2. Say, **Jesus had friends, too. His closest friends were 12 special men called "the disciples." Jesus and His disciples did everything together: they shared meals, they traveled, they helped people who were sick.**

3. Ask, **Is it always easy to be a friend? Sometimes it is hard to be loving when your friend does not treat you well.**

4. Say, **Most people think it would be easy to be Jesus' friend. Jesus was always kind and compassionate. He cared about people. He didn't take a friend's snack away; in fact, He often gave food to people who needed it.**

5. Say, **But the Bible tells us that the disciples sometimes found it hard to be Jesus' friend. They were Jesus' helpers, but they made some pretty big mistakes — even when they didn't mean to.**

6. Hide *Peter's Rooster* behind your back. Say, **One of Jesus' best friends was Peter. Peter was one of the disciples' leaders. He was noisy and energetic. Sometimes Peter said things without thinking about them. For example, he said that he would rather die than ever** say that Jesus wasn't his friend.

7. Ask, **Could you keep that promise?** Allow the children to respond. **Jesus warned Peter that this was a very hard promise to keep. Jesus was right. After Jesus was arrested, Peter pretended that he was never Jesus' friend. But he didn't just pretend once. People asked Peter three times whether or not he was Jesus' friend. Each time, Peter said, "No."**

8. Say, **After the third time, he heard a rooster crow.** Bring out *Peter's Rooster*. **That rooster reminded Peter that he had denied Jesus.**

9. Ask, **How do you think that made Jesus feel? It made Peter feel bad, too. The Bible says he wept bitterly.**

10. Ask, **How do you think Jesus treated Peter after that?** Allow the children to respond. **Let's find out what the Bible says.** Read John 21:1, 14-17. **Jesus gave Peter another chance. He asked Peter to help people follow God. How many times did He ask Peter to do this? Three times — once for each time Peter pretended he wasn't Jesus' friend. One of the wonderful things about being friends with Jesus is that He forgives us when we make mistakes.**

11. Say, **Let's pray together.** Have the children bow their heads. **Dear Lord, thank You for giving us another chance when we make mistakes. Help us to love You better. We want to be Your faithful friends. In Jesus' name, Amen.**

12. If time allows, help the children make *Peter's Roosters* as a reminder to be faithful to Jesus.

Three Is the Number All Ages

Bible Reference: Matthew 27:38; Mark 8:31; John 16:7

Overview

Three is an important number in the Easter story.

Materials

- ❑ instructions and materials for *Fruit Trios*, page 86
- ❑ three sheets of construction paper
- ❑ markers
- ❑ Bible

Preparation

1. Make a sample of *Fruit Trios*.
2. If you plan to have the children assemble *Fruit Trios*, have materials ready.
3. On one sheet of construction paper, write "Friday-1." On a second sheet, write "Saturday-2." On the third sheet, write "Sunday-3."
4. Mark Matthew 27:38, Mark 8:31 and John 16:7 in your Bible.

Presentation

1. Hold up three fingers. Ask, **How many fingers am I holding up?** (three) **Is this number special to you in any way?** (I am three years old; there are three children in my family; I have three cats.)
2. Say, **Three was a very special number to Jesus at Easter. Can you guess why?** Allow the children to brainstorm. **Those are all good guesses. Let me show you why the number three is so significant.**
3. Hold up the sample of *Fruit Trios*. Ask, **How many pieces of fruit do you see here?** (three) **These *Fruit Trios* remind me of Jesus on the cross, because on Good Friday there were actually three crosses, not one.** Read Matthew 27:38. **Jesus was put on the middle cross. There were two robbers on the other crosses. They were being punished for stealing. Jesus was being punished, but He was guilty of nothing.**
4. Say, **The *Fruit Trios* remind us that Jesus is always in the middle with us, even when we make mistakes.**
5. Ask, **How did the fruit get onto the toothpick?** (it was pierced; it was stabbed) **Jesus was pierced when He was put on the cross.**
6. Set aside the *Fruit Trios*. Lay out the three sheets of construction paper in numerical order so that the children can see them. Read Mark 8:31. Say, **Jesus said that after He died, He would be in the grave for three days.** Point to the first sheet of paper. **He died and was buried on Friday.** Point to the second paper. **He stayed in the tomb on Saturday, the Jewish Sabbath.** Point to the third paper. **On Sunday, He arose! That makes three days altogether.**
7. Say, **There is yet another way that the number three is special at Easter.** Read John 16:7. **Jesus said that when He died, He would send the Holy Spirit to be with us.** Make a triangle with your fingers. **This triangle reminds us that there are three sides of God.** Point to one side of the triangle. **God the Father sent Jesus to us.** Point to a second side. **Jesus died for us.** Point to the third side. **The Holy Spirit came to live in us.**
8. Ask, **Can anyone now tell me now why the number three is so special at Easter?** (there were three crosses; Jesus was in the grave for three days; we see the Father, Son and Holy Spirit.)
9. Say, **Let's pray together.** Have the children bow their heads. **Lord, thank You for the three crosses, the three days and the three ways we see You at Easter. In Jesus' name, Amen.**
10. If time allows, help the children to construct and sample *Fruit Trios*.

Reproducibles & Patterns

1. GAMES
2. CRAFTS
3. PUZZLES

Prayer Checklist

This list will help you pray for your event from start to finish.

Praise God for:

- ❑ The Good News of Easter morning
- ❑ The opportunity to share the Easter message with your community
- ❑ The willingness of your congregation to try a new program

Seek from God:

- ❑ Prayer partners who will pray faithfully for the event
- ❑ Wisdom about choosing a date for your event
- ❑ Insight about whom to ask to be on your team
- ❑ Certainty about which games, crafts and activities to include
- ❑ Discernment to choose effective publicity tools
- ❑ The ability to remember many details as you organize the event

Ask God for:

- ❑ Enough willing helpers
- ❑ A loving, caring atmosphere among your workers
- ❑ Adequate funds and contributions
- ❑ A spirit of cooperation and anticipation during the set-up time
- ❑ Good weather
- ❑ Safety for all participants
- ❑ Many new families to be reached
- ❑ Open hearts during the Easter story presentation
- ❑ Your church to grow as the result of this event

Intercede for:

- ❑ The volunteer training sessions
- ❑ The volunteers who greet visitors at the registration table
- ❑ Those supervising games, crafts and activities
- ❑ Those helpers sharing the Easter story
- ❑ Congregation members who will invite neighbors and friends
- ❑ Families and children receiving invitations
- ❑ Your pastor as he or she greets guests

After the Celebration:

- ❑ Praise God for the successes of the day
- ❑ Ask God to show you how to correct any weaknesses for next year
- ❑ Thank Him for your volunteers
- ❑ Intercede for unchurched guests
- ❑ Pray that your congregation will reach out to visitors who return for worship

Help bring the Easter message to our community!

I can help the day of the event _____
(event date and time)

Name	Phone	Job
_____	_____	_____
_____	_____	_____
_____	_____	_____
_____	_____	_____
_____	_____	_____

I can help set up for the event on _____.
(set up date and time)

Name	Phone	Job
_____	_____	_____
_____	_____	_____
_____	_____	_____
_____	_____	_____
_____	_____	_____

I can help cut out and prepare craft supplies and games prior to the event.

Name	Phone	Job
_____	_____	_____
_____	_____	_____
_____	_____	_____
_____	_____	_____
_____	_____	_____

Volunteer Training Checklist

Use this checklist to help you prepare your volunteers for your event.

All volunteers need to:

- ❏ Greet participants in a friendly way
- ❏ Know the activity schedule
- ❏ Know where various activities will be located

Registration table volunteers need to:

- ❏ Know how to fill out the registration form for each child
- ❏ Invite each registered child to participate in the *Jelly Bean Guessing Game*
- ❏ Give each child a take-home bag and registration packet
- ❏ Show each child where to go to begin

Crafts and games volunteers need to:

- ❏ Know how to do their craft or play their game
- ❏ Know approximately how long their craft or game takes to do
- ❏ Have supplies or prizes ready

Face painting and balloon hat volunteers need to:

- ❏ Select a few designs to use
- ❏ Practice those designs
- ❏ Have supplies ready

Petting zoo volunteers need to:

- ❏ Arrange a quiet place for the animals
- ❏ Show children how to be gentle with the animals

Snack Volunteers need to:

- ❏ Know how to prepare the snack
- ❏ Show children where to wash their hands

The Easter Bunny needs to:

- ❏ Wear his costume
- ❏ Circulate unobtrusively
- ❏ Have a basket of goodies to share with the children

Volunteers taking photos need to:

- ❏ Have plenty of fresh film
- ❏ Know the kinds of photos you want
- ❏ Keep a record of whose photo has been taken

Piñata volunteers need to:

- ❏ Have a bat and blindfold for each piñata
- ❏ Ensure that the children are safe

Volunteers hiding eggs need to:

- ❏ Know where to hide the eggs
- ❏ Know how many eggs to hide

Volunteers leading the singing need to:

- ❏ Know what songs to present
- ❏ Have the words available on overhead projector or in hymnal

Volunteers presenting the Easter story need to:

- ❏ Practice the presentation
- ❏ Have materials ready

Volunteers making follow up visits need to:

- ❏ Thank visitors for attending
- ❏ Ask if they have any needs your church can meet
- ❏ Invite visitors to worship

Supply Checklist

Publicity

- ❏ Bulletin inserts and publicity flyers
- ❏ Posters
- ❏ Postcards and current mailing list
- ❏ Prizes for congregation invitation contest
- ❏ Announcement for local media
- ❏ Outside banner

Registration

- ❏ Registration forms and pencils
- ❏ Take-home bags, schedule of events, church layout/map, church brochure
- ❏ Visitor evaluation forms
- ❏ Jelly beans, *Jelly Bean Guessing Game**

Decorations and Set-up

- ❏ Balloons, helium tank, ribbon or string*
- ❏ Crepe paper streamers*
- ❏ Additional decorations
- ❏ Directional signs

Games and Crafts

- ❏ Game supplies for those selected from pages 36-55
- ❏ Prizes*
- ❏ Prize boxes or baskets for each station*
- ❏ Craft supplies for those selected from pages 56-81
- ❏ Large basket or box to collect congregation's donations

Other Activities

- ❏ Face paints*
- ❏ Pencil balloons, balloon pump*
- ❏ Easter Bunny costume, basket of treats*
- ❏ Petting zoo animals
- ❏ Piñatas, rope, blindfolds, bats, wrapped candies and prizes*
- ❏ Easter story book, costumes, props, *Resurrection Eggs*
- ❏ Plastic Easter eggs, wrapped candies*
- ❏ Film for photos, plastic Easter eggs, wrapped candies*

*Designates supplies that are easy for congregation members to donate. List them in your church bulletin and newsletter. See page 118 for a sample supply donation form.

Help reach our community at Easter!

We are sponsoring an **Easter Celebration** for the children of our community on

_____.
(date)

Can you help by donating some of these items?

Please place them in the baskets located _____

_____
(location of supplies collection)

by _____.
(date)

We need:
(list needed supplies here)

THANK YOU!

- -

Bulletin Insert

Easter Celebration for Kids!

Ages 3 through Grade 5

_____

_____

_____
(date, time, location)

Bring a friend!

Easter Egg Hunt

Games and Prizes

Crafts

Singing

Story Time

FREE!

Bring your Easter basket!

Pre-registration is encouraged

Please call _____
(church office)

Come join us!

 # Easter Celebration

For Kids
Ages 3 through Grade 5

_____
(date)

_____
(time)

_____
(church name)

Easter Egg Hunt

Games & Prizes

Crafts

Singing

Story Time

FREE!

Pre-Registration encouraged

Please call _____
(church phone)

_____
(church location)

Bring your Easter basket & join us!

Children through age 6 require adult supervision.

Egg pattern

Cross pattern

Registration Form

Child's Name:_____

Date of Birth: _____

Grade in School: _____

Parents' Names:_____

Child's Address: _____

Home Phone: _____

Home Church?_____

Person to call in an emergency:_____

Emergency Phone: _____

How did you hear about us? _____

Thank you for joining us!

Our Easter celebration is coming...
and **YOU** are invited!

Date: _____

Time: _____

Place: _____

Games • Crafts • Piñatas
Prizes • Stories

And an eggs-traordinary **egg hunt!**

FREE!

Pre-registration encouraged at:_____

_____

Adult supervision required for
children ages 6 and under.

Bring your Easter Basket!

GOOD FOR 1 SNACK	GOOD FOR 1 SNACK
GOOD FOR 1 SNACK	GOOD FOR 1 SNACK
GOOD FOR 1 SNACK	GOOD FOR 1 SNACK
GOOD FOR 1 SNACK	GOOD FOR 1 SNACK
GOOD FOR 1 SNACK	GOOD FOR 1 SNACK
GOOD FOR 1 SNACK	GOOD FOR 1 SNACK
GOOD FOR 1 SNACK	GOOD FOR 1 SNACK

ADMIT 1 TO EGG HUNT	**ADMIT 1 TO EGG HUNT**
ADMIT 1 TO EGG HUNT	**ADMIT 1 TO EGG HUNT**
ADMIT 1 TO EGG HUNT	**ADMIT 1 TO EGG HUNT**
ADMIT 1 TO EGG HUNT	**ADMIT 1 TO EGG HUNT**
ADMIT 1 TO EGG HUNT	**ADMIT 1 TO EGG HUNT**
ADMIT 1 TO EGG HUNT	**ADMIT 1 TO EGG HUNT**
ADMIT 1 TO EGG HUNT	**ADMIT 1 TO EGG HUNT**

Visitor Evaluation

Thank you for joining us for our **Easter celebration**! Please take a few minutes and answer the questions below. We would like your feedback so that we can effectively minister to children and families.

1. What was your child's favorite activity? _____

2. Which activity did your child enjoy least? _____

3. Were you satisfied with the quality and variety of activities for children? _____

4. Was the message of Easter evident to you and your family? _____

5. Was the event organized and staffed to your satisfaction? _____

6. Would you come again? _____

7. How did you hear about our event? _____

Additional Comments: _____

_____

Thank you for your response. **Happy Easter!**

He is not here; He has risen! ~ Matthew 28:6

Volunteer Evaluation

Thank you for helping with our Easter celebration!
Please take a few minutes and answer the questions below.
We would like your feedback so that we can effectively minister to children and families.

1. Which activities worked best? Why? _____

2. Which activities were least effective? Why? _____

3. Were you satisfied with the variety, volume and quality of activities presented? Why or why not?

_____

4. Were you satisfied with the organization and preparation put into the event?_____

5. Did you receive adequate training/instruction to complete your task?_____

6. What could we do better next year? _____

7. Would you participate again? _____

Additional Comments: _____

_____

Thank you for your response. **Happy Easter!**
He is not here; He has risen! ~ Matthew 28:6

Set-up Checklist

Prior to Set-up

❏ Decide where to locate each station

❏ Reproduce instructions for each activity you are using

❏ Collect necessary supplies

❏ Construct needed game parts

❏ Make a *Beautiful Badge* (page 57) for each volunteer

❏ Duplicate volunteer evaluation form, visitor evaluation form and snack and egg hunt tickets

❏ Have extra *Registration Forms* and church brochures on hand

Set-up Time

❏ Set up registration table

❏ Make registration packets to include take-home bags, registration forms, church brochures, name tags, snack tickets, facility map, schedule of events and visitor evaluation forms

❏ Arrange tables at each station

❏ Set up chairs for volunteers and visiting parents

❏ Post map of facility, traffic flow signs and schedule of events

❏ Make a poster for each station

❏ Give each volunteer the written instructions for his or her station

❏ Distribute supplies to each station

❏ Have craft volunteers make a sample craft

❏ Have game volunteers play games

❏ Have snack volunteers make a sample snack

❏ Rehearse Easter story

❏ Stuff Easter eggs

❏ Stuff piñatas

❏ Decorate facility

❏ Designate hunting areas for the egg hunt

❏ Give each volunteer a *Beautiful Badge*

Welcome to our
EASTER CELEBRATION

at _____
(church name)

Schedule of Events

10:00 a.m.	Registration & Jellybean Guessing Game
10:00-11:00 a.m.	Games, Crafts & additional activities
11:00-11:15 a.m.	Piñatas

Ages 3-5: _____
(location)

Ages 6-8: _____
(location)

Ages 9-12: _____
(location)

11:20-11:40 a.m.	Singing, Easter Story & Announcements
11:45 a.m. - Noon	Easter Egg Hunt
	(Children will be escorted in age groups to specific hunting areas.)

Thank you for coming today! Jesus loves you!

Follow-up letter

Dear Friend:

Thank you for attending the Easter celebration at [church name]. We were delighted to have you as our guests as we celebrate Jesus' resurrection.

We invite you to join us on Easter Sunday at [time] as we worship together. In addition, our Sunday school meets at [time] with classes for all ages, and we love to see new faces.

We also minister to families through our [list ministry opportunities]. If your children enjoyed our Easter celebration then they will also want to participate in our [vacation Bible school or next available children's event].

Please contact our church office at [church telephone number] for further information about these programs. We look forward to seeing you again!

In Christ,
(signed)
Easter Celebration Director
(signed)
Pastor

Butterfly Mosaics pattern

Sunshine Smiles pattern

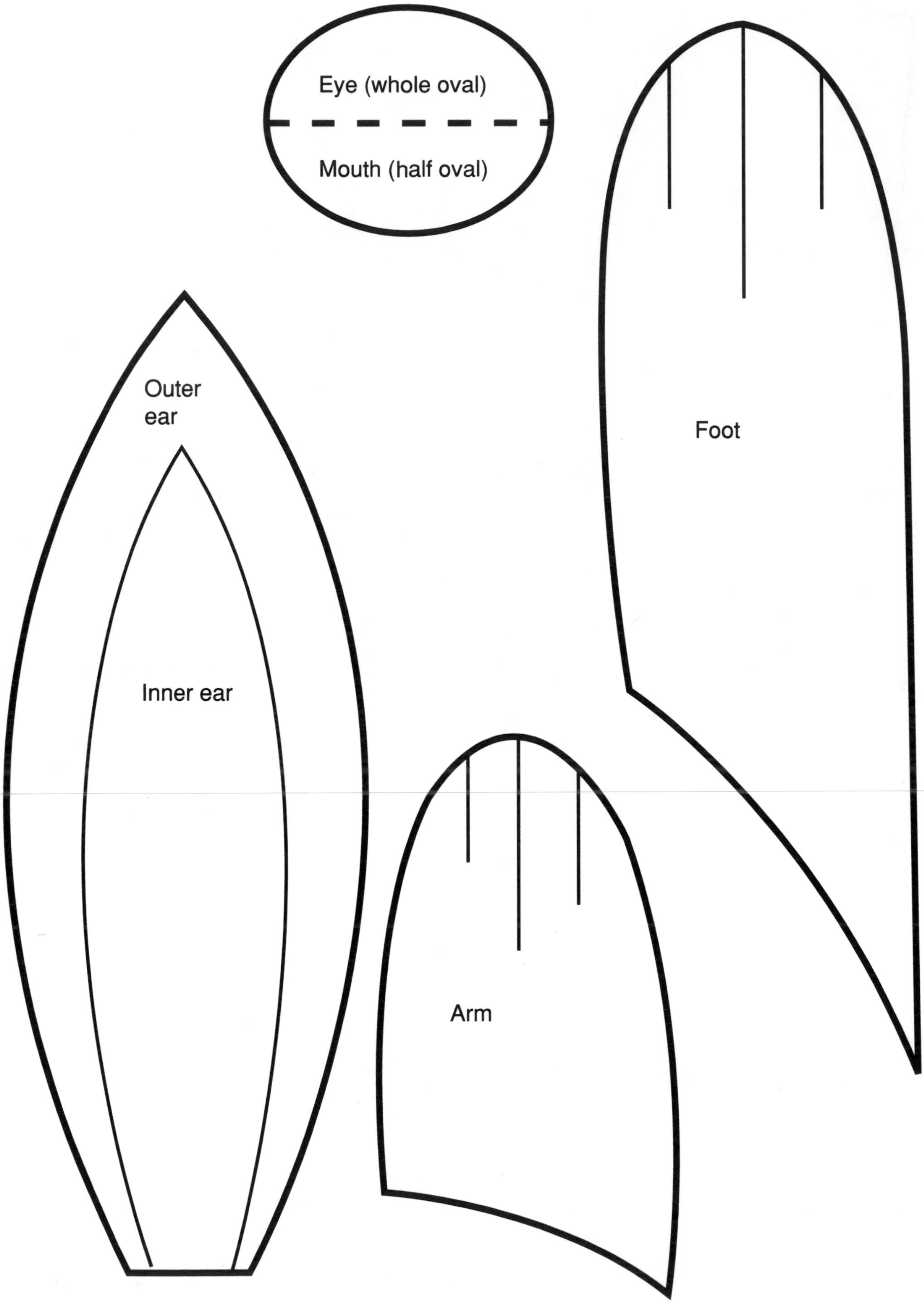

Eye (whole oval)

Mouth (half oval)

Outer
ear

Inner ear

Foot

Arm

Carrot Toss patterns

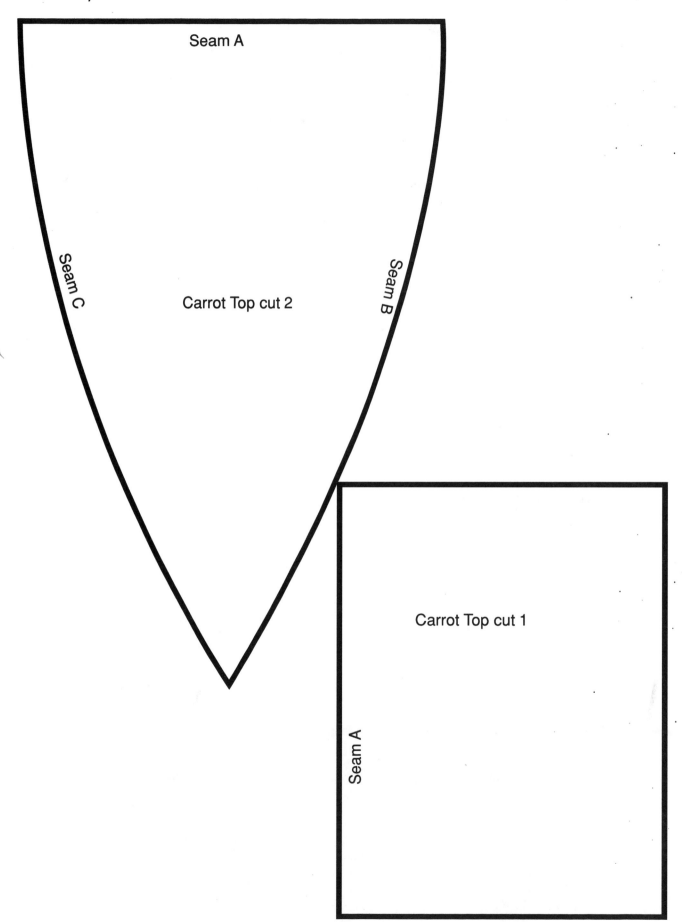

Seam A

Seam C

Carrot Top cut 2

Seam B

Carrot Top cut 1

Seam A

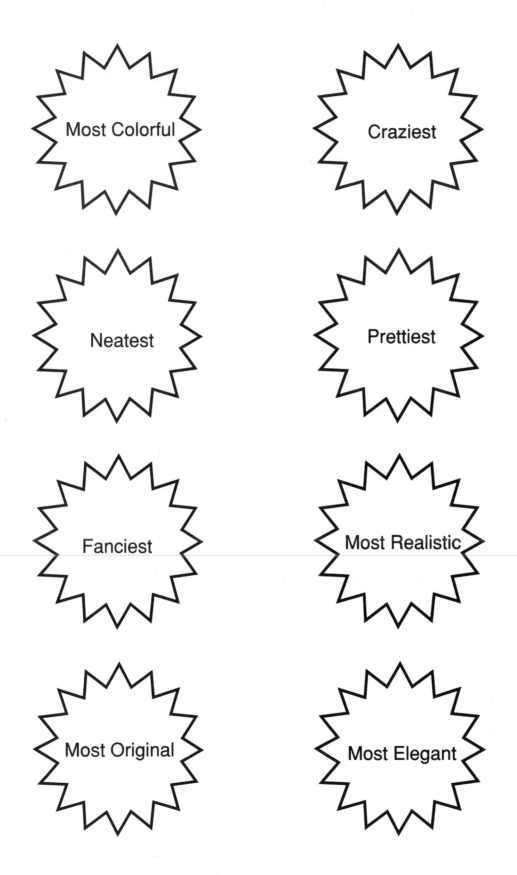

Most Colorful

Craziest

Neatest

Prettiest

Fanciest

Most Realistic

Most Original

Most Elegant

Coloring Contest pattern
Eggshell Mosaic pattern

HE IS NOT

HERE,

HE HAS

RISEN!

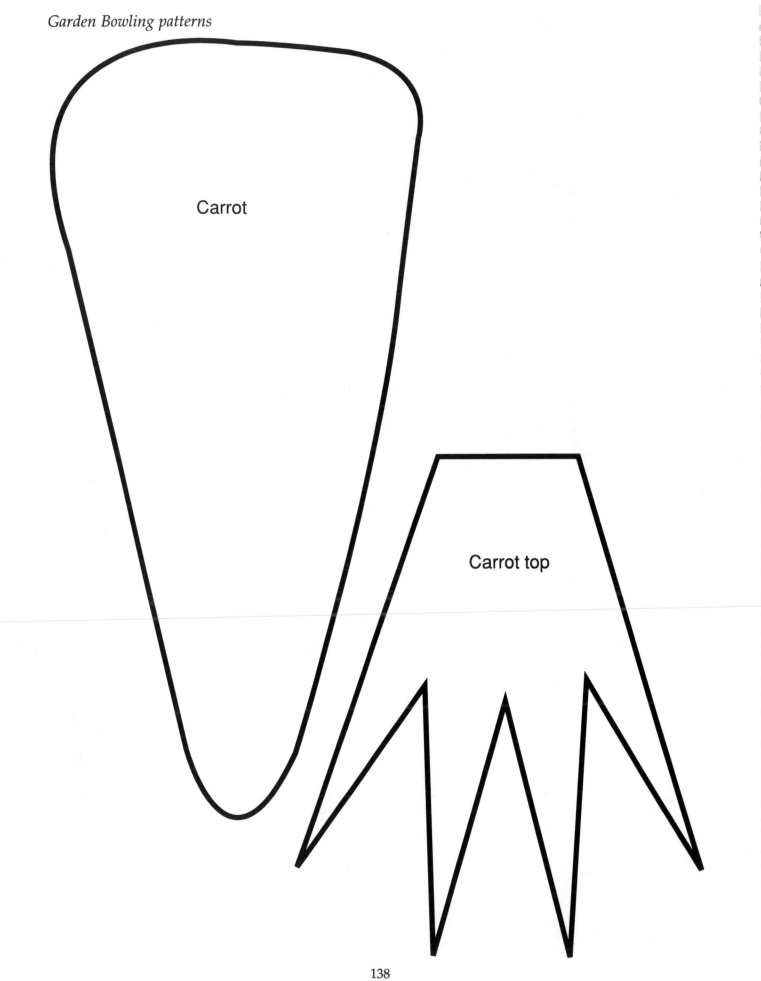

Carrot

Carrot top

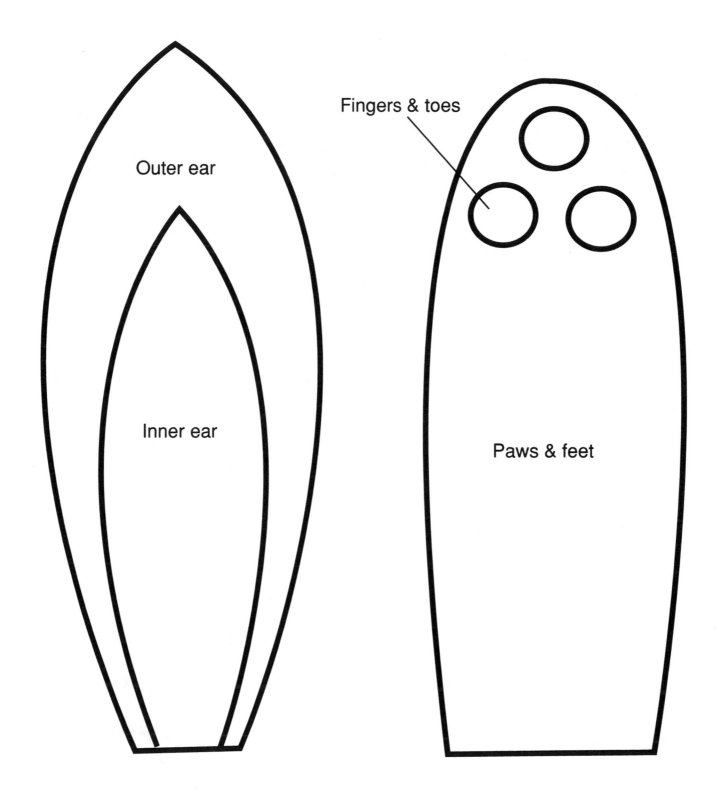

Outer ear

Inner ear

Fingers & toes

Paws & feet

Pin the Palm Branch patterns

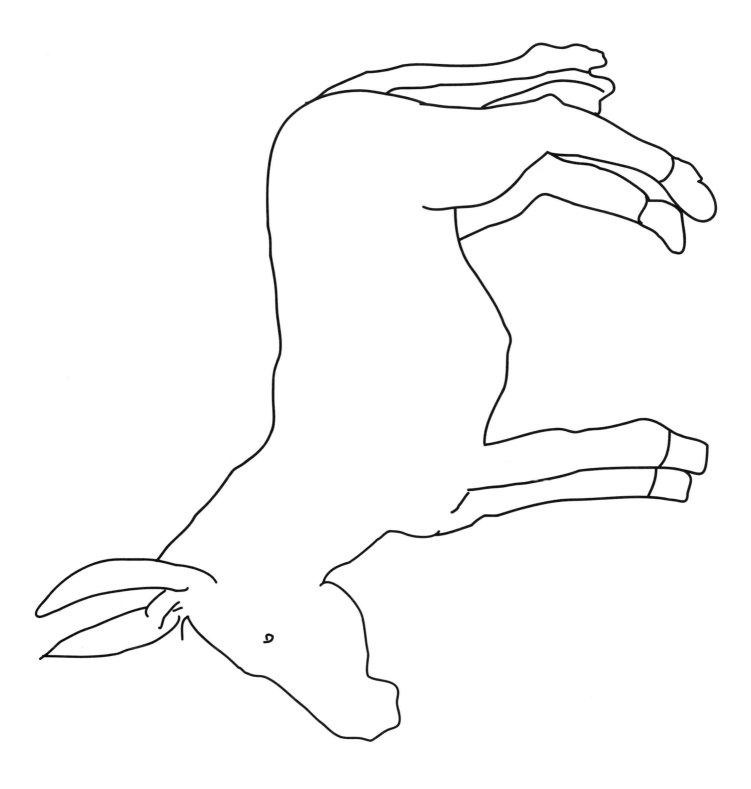

The Way to the Cross pattern

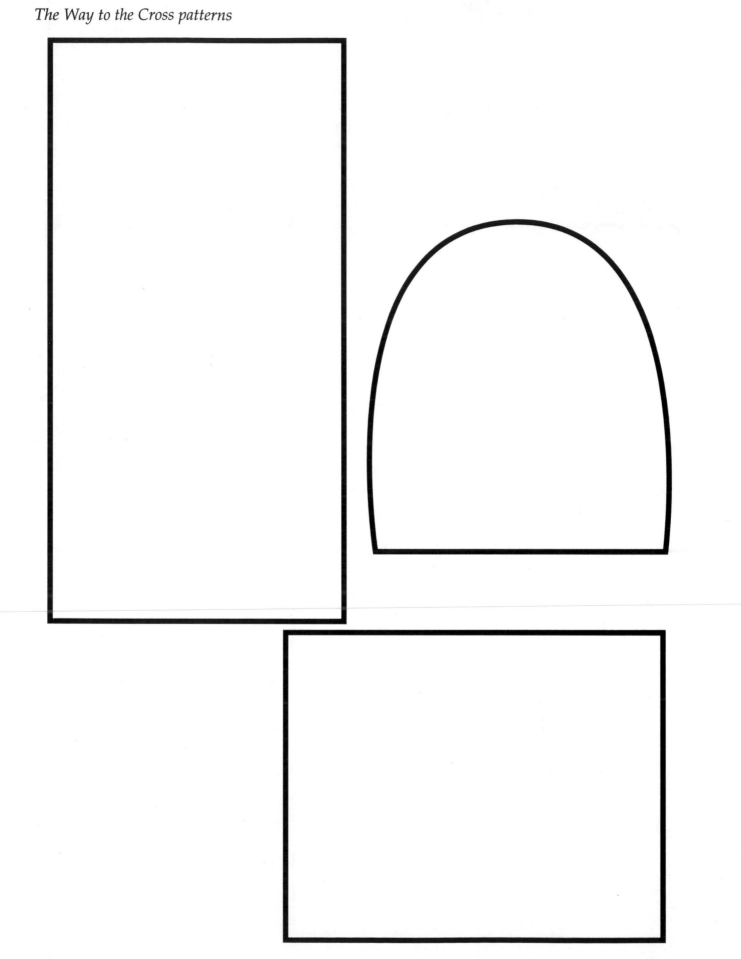

PETER	**ANDREW**
JAMES	**JOHN**
PHILIP	**BARTHOLOMEW**
THOMAS	**MATTHEW**
JAMES	**THADDEUS**
SIMON	**JUDAS**

Responses to kids playing game:

- Peter: leader of the disciples; called the "rock"
- Andrew: introduced people to Jesus; brought boy with loaves and fishes to Jesus at feeding of 5,000
- James: one of Jesus' closest friends
- John: wrote a book in the Bible
- Philip: decided to follow Jesus after hearing John the Baptist preach
- Bartholomew: became a missionary to India
- Thomas: doubted, but was a courageous disciple
- Matthew: left his job as a tax collector to follow Jesus
- James: one of two disciples with the same name
- Thaddaeus: also called "Lebbaeus"
- Simon: was a Zealot, a type of political group

Bunny Bag patterns

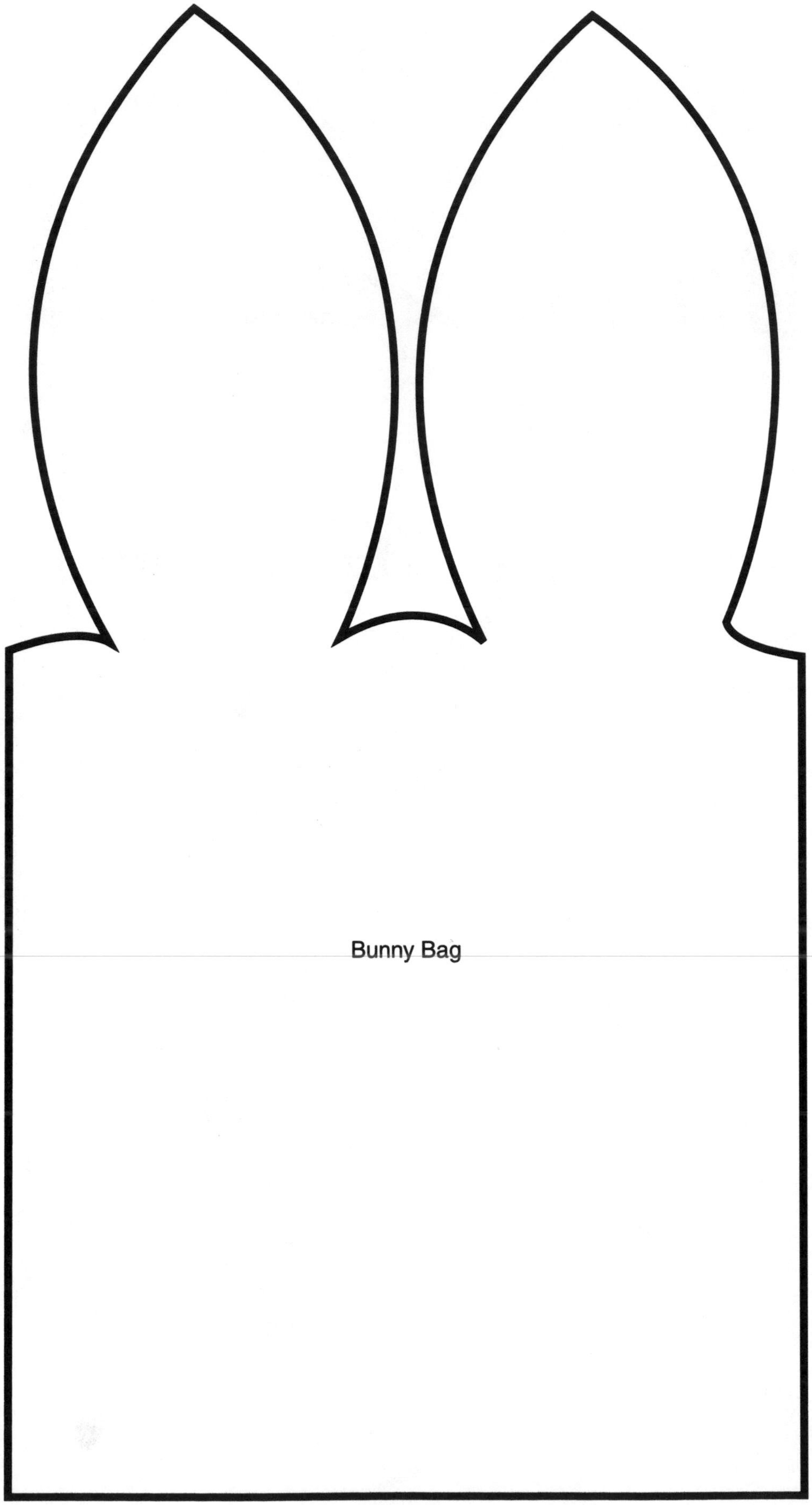

Bunny Bag

Mouth

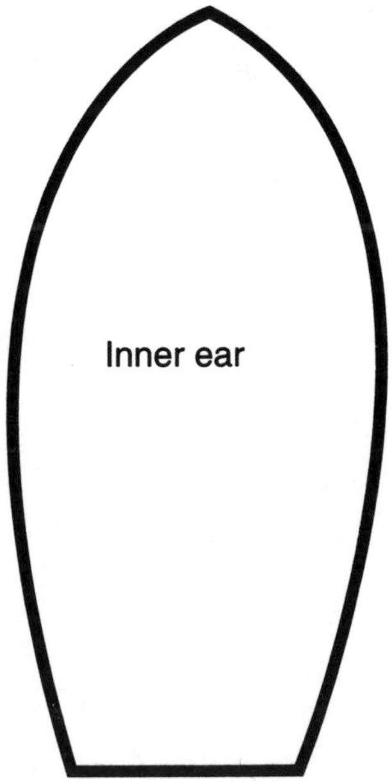

Inner ear

Bunny Ears pattern

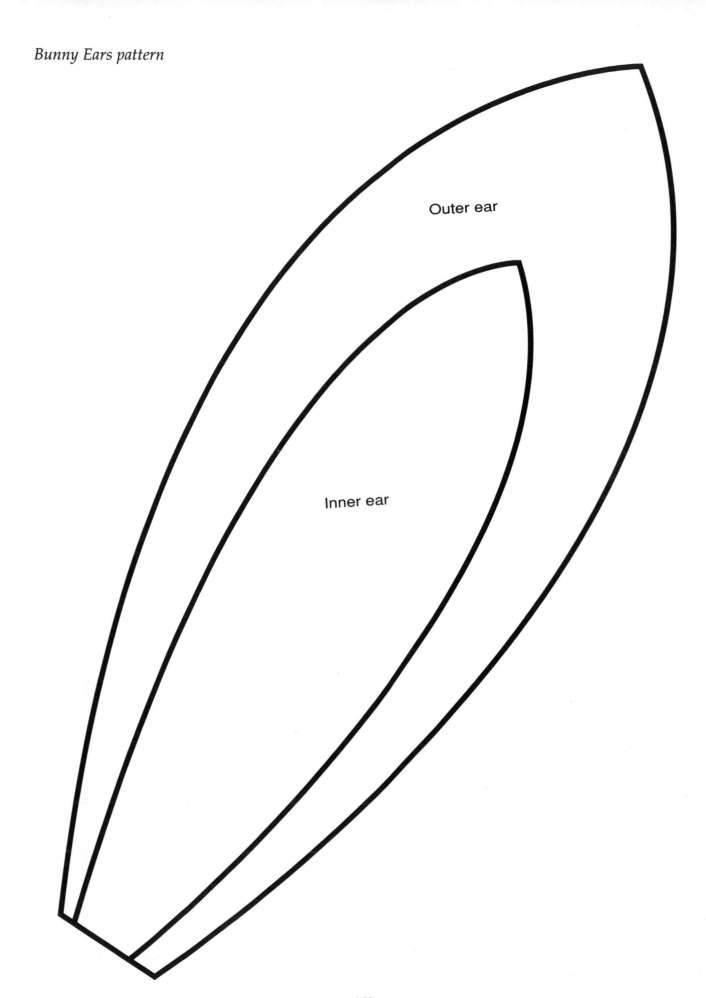

Outer ear

Inner ear

Wings

Body

Bookmark

Chick Pencil Topper patterns

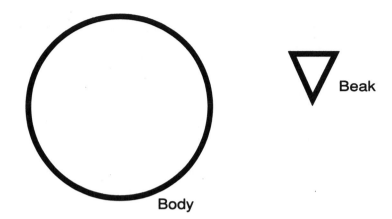

Beak

Body

Cotton Ball Sheep pattern

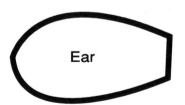

Ear

Cottontail Basket pattern

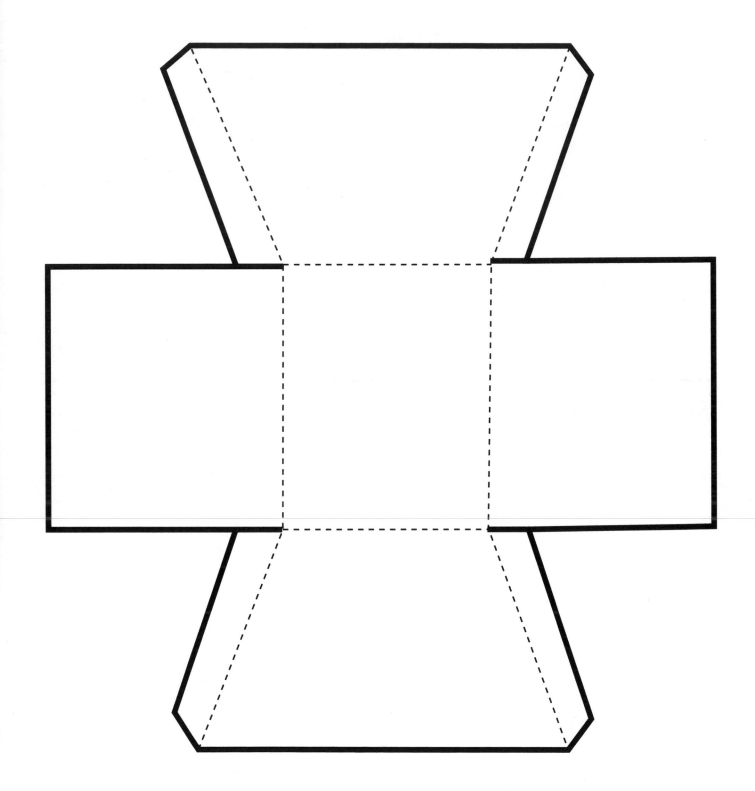

Cottontail Basket patterns

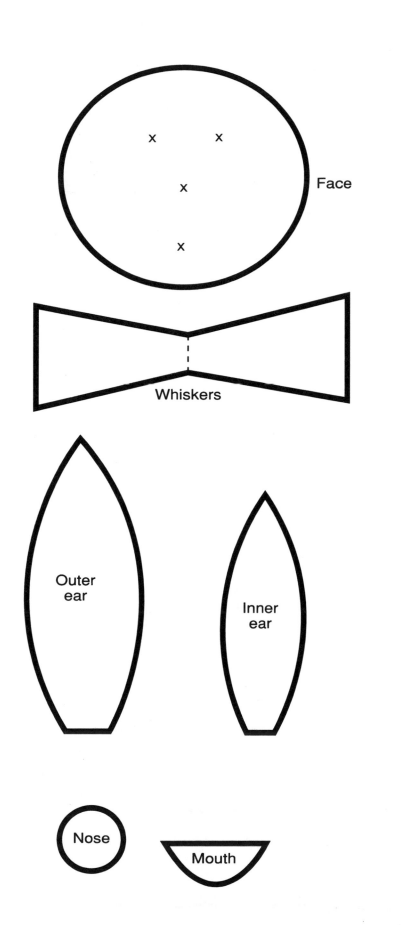

Face

Whiskers

Outer
ear

Inner
ear

Nose

Mouth

Handle

Duct Tape Donkey patterns

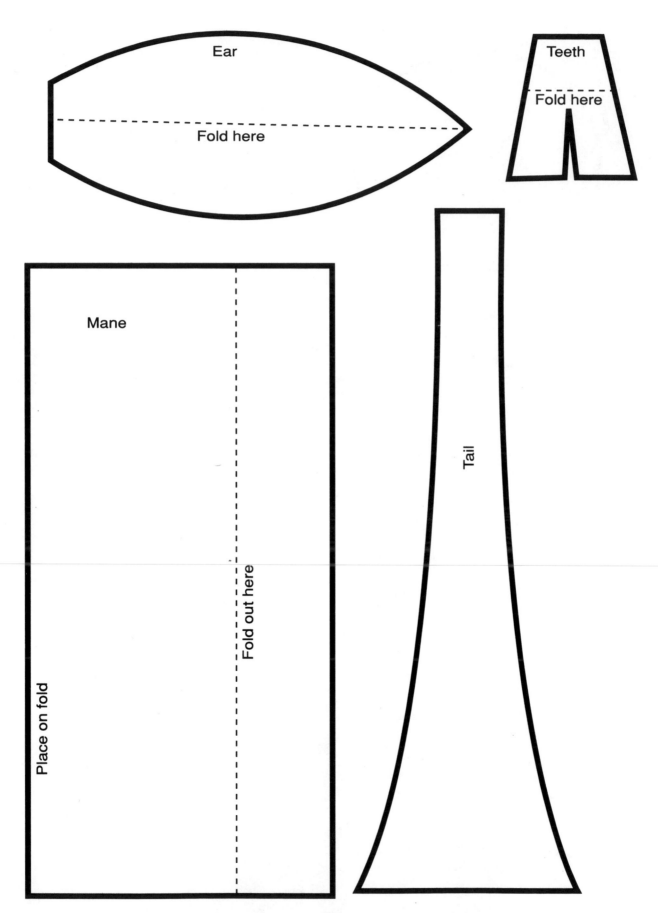

Ear

Fold here

Teeth

Fold here

Mane

Place on fold

Fold out here

Tail

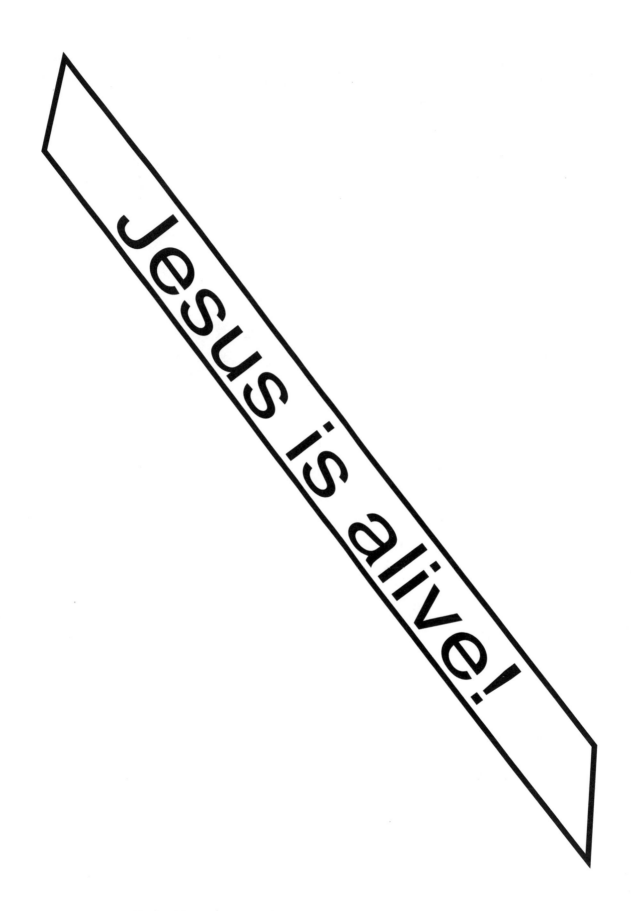

Jesus is alive!

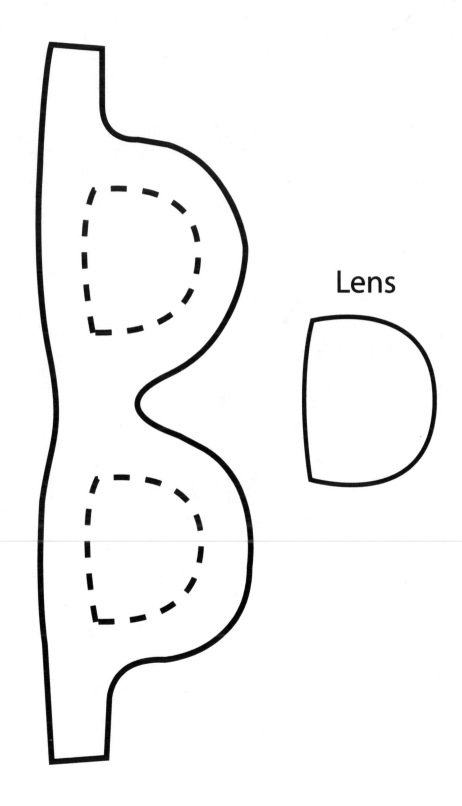

Lens

Gumstick Butterfly patterns

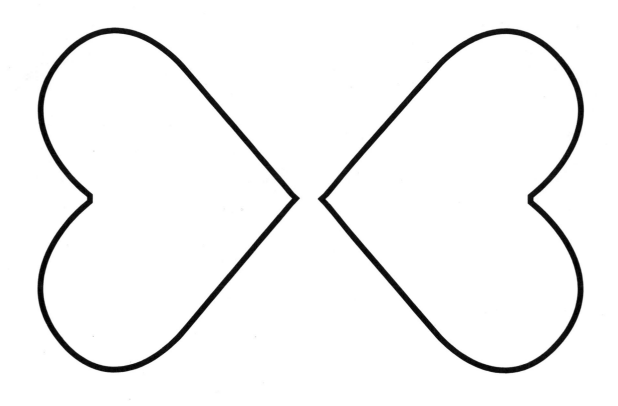

Love Bank patterns

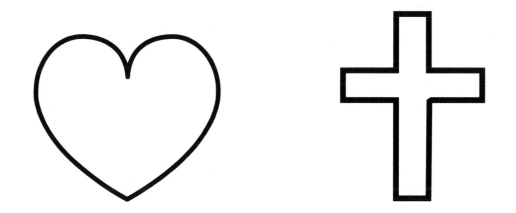

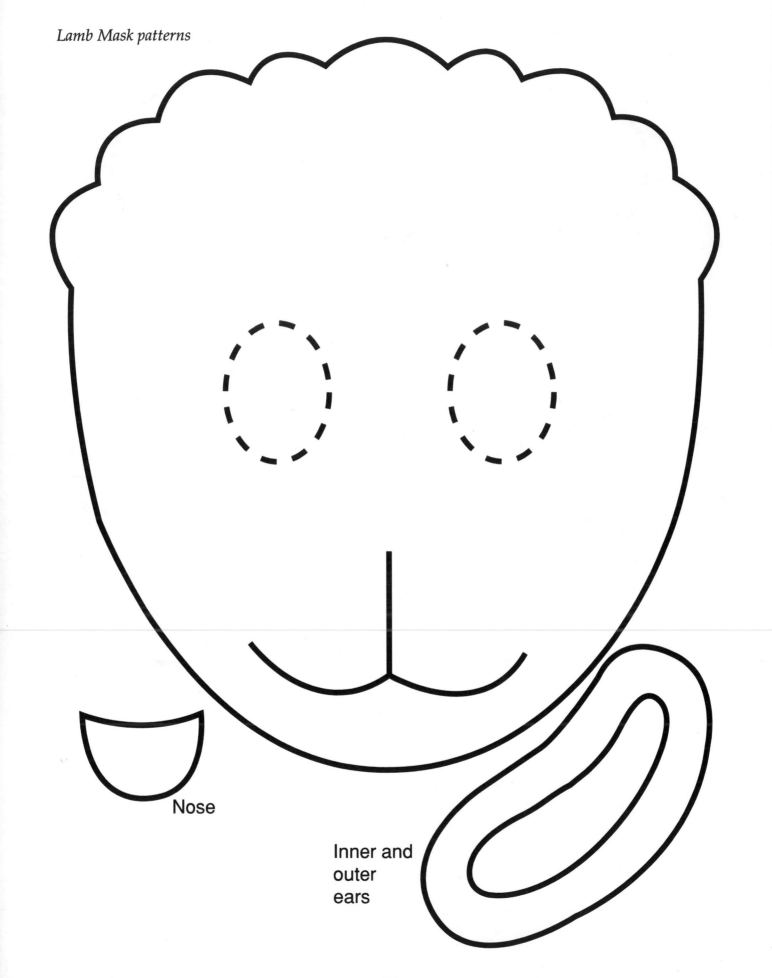

Lamb Mask patterns

Nose

Inner and
outer
ears

Peter's Rooster pattern

Resurrection Rainbow pattern

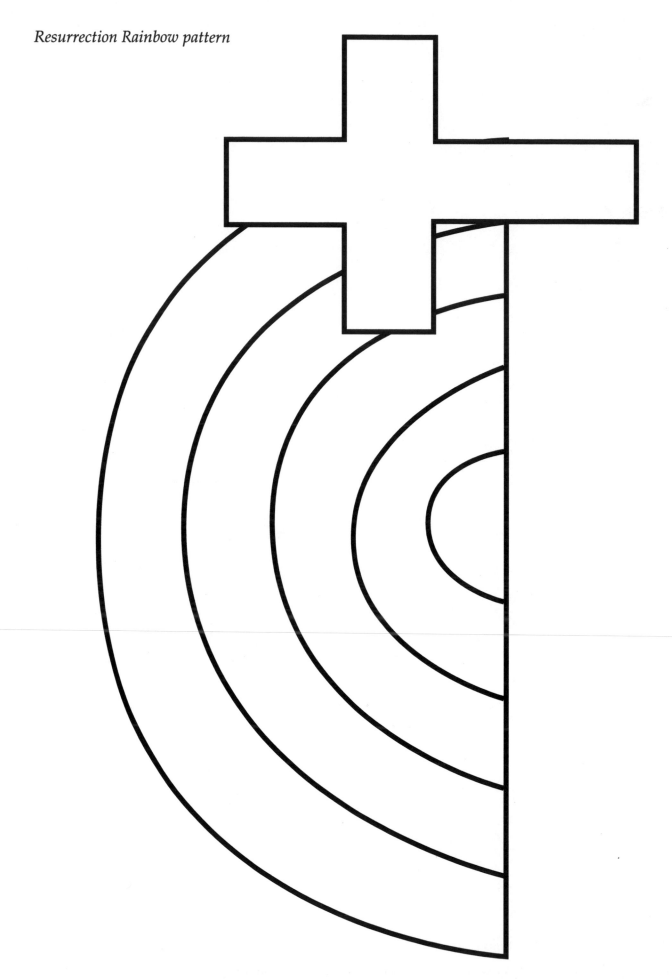

Salvation Story

First Knot: Reminds us of when we were physically born (John 3:3-6)

Black: Reminds us that we are all sinners and make mistakes (Romans 3:23)

Red: Reminds us that Jesus paid for those mistakes by dying on the cross (Romans 5:8)

White: Reminds us that we are forgiven and cleansed because of Jesus (Isaiah 1:18)

Blue: Reminds us of the water used when we are baptized (Acts 2:41)

Green: Reminds us to grow closer to God by praying, reading the Bible and attending church (Colossians 1:10)

Yellow: Reminds us of the glory of heaven, when we will be with Jesus (Revelation 21:1-4)

Second Knot: Reminds us that one day our lives will end and we will meet God (Hebrews 9:27)

Clear: Reminds us of Jesus' clear call to put our faith in Him (John 3:16)

Salvation Story

First Knot: Reminds us of when we were physically born (John 3:3-6)

Black: Reminds us that we are all sinners and make mistakes (Romans 3:23)

Red: Reminds us that Jesus paid for those mistakes by dying on the cross (Romans 5:8)

White: Reminds us that we are forgiven and cleansed because of Jesus (Isaiah 1:18)

Blue: Reminds us of the water used when we are baptized (Acts 2:41)

Green: Reminds us to grow closer to God by praying, reading the Bible and attending church (Colossians 1:10)

Yellow: Reminds us of the glory of heaven, when we will be with Jesus (Revelation 21:1-4)

Second Knot: Reminds us that one day our lives will end and we will meet God (Hebrews 9:27)

Clear: Reminds us of Jesus' clear call to put our faith in Him (John 3:16)

Spring Flower Basket patterns

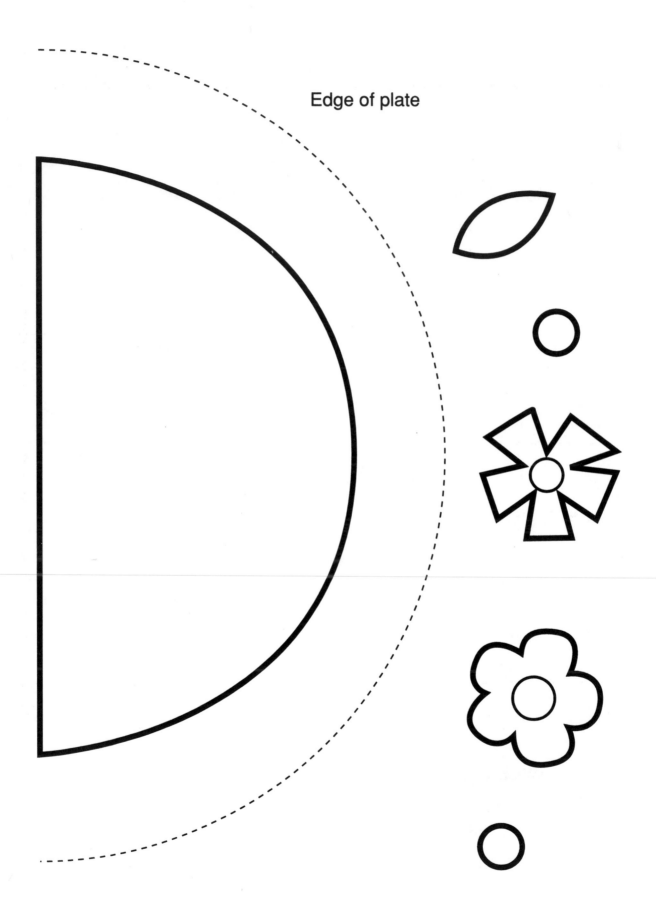

Edge of plate

Tissue Paper Flowers pattern
Wallpaper Butterfly pattern (upper wings)

Wallpaper Butterfly pattern (lower wings)

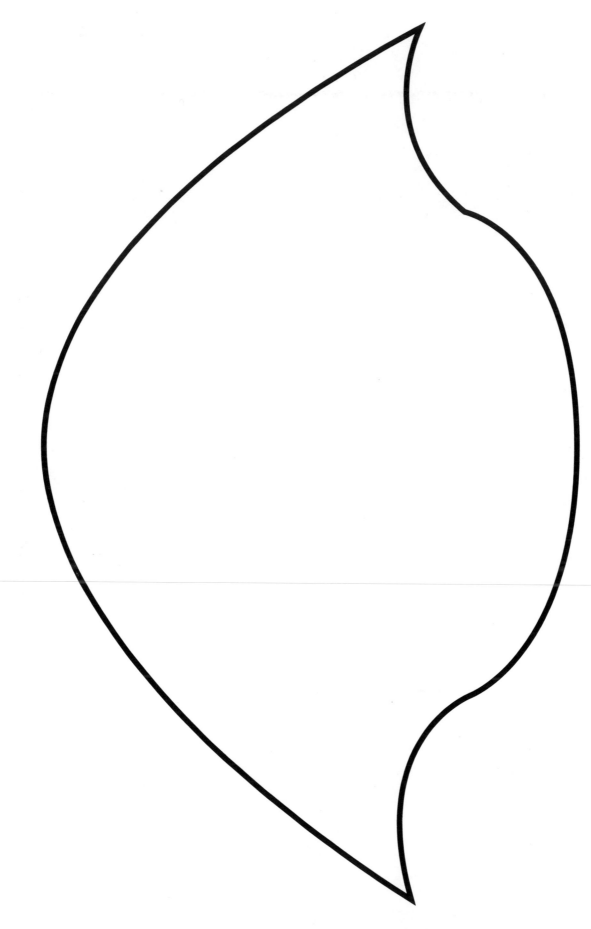

Scripture Reference Index

Sources

Badges

Badge-A-Minit
(800) 223-4103
FAX: (815) 883-9696

Balloon Supplies and Resources

Wisdom Clubs International
P.O. Box 1585
Sandy, OR 97055
(503) 668-0101

Piccadilly Books
P.O. Box 25203
Colorado Springs, CO 80936

Craft Supplies

Oriental Trading Company, Inc.
P.O. Box 2308
Omaha, NE 68103-0407
(800) 228-2269
www.oriental.com

Really Good Stuff
The Cinema Center
Botsford, CT 06404-0386
(800) 366-1920
www.reallygoodstuff.com

S & S Christian Crafts
P.O. Box 513
Colchester, CT
06415-0513
(800) 243-9232
FAX: (800) 566-6678
www.snswwide.com

Flannel Graph Supplies

Betty Lukens, Inc.
711 Portal Street
Cotati, CA 94931
(800) 541-9279
FAX: (800) 795-8225
www.bettylukens.com

Prizes and Novelties

Current
Colorado Springs, CO 80941-0001
(800) 767-2766
FAX: (800) 993-3232
www.currentcatalog.com

Fun Stuff
P.O. Box 2600
Forrester Center, WV 25438-4306
(877) 222-2FUN
www.funstuff4u.com

Inspirations
P.O. Box 2659
Omaha, NE 68103-2659
(800) 228-2269
www.oriental.com

Oriental Trading Company, Inc.
P.O. Box 2308
Omaha, NE 68103-0407
(800) 228-2269
www.oriental.com

Resurrection Eggs

FamilyLife
3900 North Rodney Parham
Little Rock, AR 72212
(501) 223-8663
www.familylife-ccc.com